WOOD
THROUGH
WATER

WOOD THROUGH WATER

CLASSIC POWER BOATS

JAMES W. OGILVIE KNOWLES   JUSTUS HAYES

FRIEDMAN/FAIRFAX

A FRIEDMAN/FAIRFAX BOOK
© 2002 by Michael Friedman Publishing Group, Inc.

Please visit our website: www.metrobooks.com

Library of Congress Cataloging-in-Publication Data available upon request.

ISBN 1-58663-565-4

Editor: Ann Kirby
Art Director: Kevin Ullrich
Designer: Lynne Yeamans
Photography Editor: Valerie Kennedy

Color separations by Colourscan Overseas Co. Pte Ltd.
Printed in China by Leefung-Asco Printers Ltd.

1 3 5 7 9 10 8 6 4 2

Distributed by Sterling Publishing Company, Inc.
387 Park Avenue South
New York, NY 10016
Distributed in Canada by Sterling Publishing
Canadian Manda Group
One Atlantic Avenue, Suite 105
Toronto, Ontario, Canada M6K 3E7
Distributed in Australia by
Capricorn Link (Australia) Pty, Ltd.
P.O. Box 704, Windsor, NSW 2756 Australia

D e d i c a t i o n s

This book was written for the late William G. Ogilvie, who gave me my love of the sea, and in memory of Annette "C.J." O'Reilly, with love to my children, Ashley, Tanysha, and Helyna.

—James W. Ogilvie Knowles

I dedicate my part in this book to my love, Aileen. Thanks for your patience and support, and the occasional kick in the pants. I needed all of them.

—Justus Hayes

Contents

I have spent my entire life in and around wooden boats. From my childhood years on Lake Muskoka to my grown-up obsession with rebuilding and restoring vintage boats, I have been surrounded by boats and boating lore for as long as I can remember. My granddad was one of Canada's first Chris-Craft dealers, working in the Muskoka region of Ontario from the 1920s through to the late '60s. He was also a writer who co-authored *The Greatest Little Motor Boat Afloat,* a book on the disappearing propeller boat, and appeared regularly in the columns of the local newspapers and magazines. I've spent the past few years digging through the archive of vintage photographs, advertisements, catalogs, and boating magazines that he amassed during his long life. Yet until I began writing this book, I never really realized how much of an influence the land, water, people, and the numerous wooden boats I have seen, ridden in, and worked on have had on me.

As far back as I can remember, my mother would load my brother and I into the car and head for Muskoka; about a two-hour drive from our home in Toronto. We made countless trips throughout the year, in summer to visit Browning Island and my grandfather's boathouse, and in winter to strap on the boards and ski on what they knew locally as slopes in Muskoka. Usually, with a cat or two along for the ride, my brother Bruce and I would fight all the way up north to Gravenhurst (where we would stop to gather provisions), ducking backhands from my mother while the cats did their best to escape from this moving hell called a "car."

My fondest memories of those times always take me back to Campbell's Landing on the southeast side of Lake Muskoka. There, the three-hour ordeal would end. My brother and I would wait eagerly at the dock, knowing that after a while, "Grandpa Boo" would appear from some distant part of the lake in one or another sleek, fast boat. From open cockpit utilities to triple cockpit runabouts, my granddad, as one of the foremost boat dealers and builders in Eastern Canada, was always driving a different type of boat. The fact that he didn't own the boats never occurred to us at the time; we assumed that each and every one of those powerful, elegant vessels was his and his alone.

He would appear first as a small white spot out in the lake, which would get bigger and bigger as the craft came forward toward Campbell's Landing. Growing larger, the white ball of spray seemed to blossom as the shiny mahogany bow peered now and then through the flying water. My brother and I would jump up and down and strain our eyes with great anticipation, then excitement at the realization that behind the wheel of the speeding craft was indeed our Grandpa Boo. With a broad welcome wave of a hand he would make the turn into the dock. More often than not he would come along side (the driver's side), seemingly without moving a muscle or flinching an eye. The only movement you would see as he wheeled the powerful boat up to the dock was his arm reaching out to grab for a hold on the wooden structure, calmly bringing the vessel to a stop at our feet. Mom would jump in first so my brother and I could hand the groceries and the cats down to her.

As long as the car ride had seemed, the ride across the lake in the speeding craft would always feel far too short. It was heaven to sit back in the aft cockpit of one of those powerful and classy machines, with Boo throttling up and Mom shouting over the rumble of the engine and the yowling of the cats, "For heaven's sake, slow it down!" When we eventually did slow down, it would be for the final approach to the old wooden boathouse that sat out on a point in its own bay on Browning Island. The boathouse, with its starboard side hanging well out over the water, seemed to be precariously perched upon the flat, moss-covered rocks of Muskoka. Most of the building was out over the water, and as we came around the front of the wooden structure the dark gaping mouth of the entrance bid us welcome. Displaying the same expert ability landing the craft that he did at Campbell's Landing, Grandpa Boo would give the engine just enough throttle to come around the point, and glide it to a halt inside the darkness of the weathered boathouse.

At the end of the day, we would be sent to bed after having our usual fight over who would have to sleep in the top bunk, where wharf spiders were known to lurk in vast numbers. But if we weren't too worn out, Bruce and I would get up and sneak out into the hall that encircled the building on the second floor. Crawling to the edge, we would look below at the profile of the wooden craft, glistening in the reflection of the lamp burning in the kitchen window. The warm glow of light jumping off the glossy hardwood always seemed magical.

It is that sense of magic that makes wooden powerboats—from tiny launches to big, brawny sportfishers—so special. There are plenty of fiberglass boats out there that will do any job just as well and perhaps more efficiently as a vintage Chris-Craft, Gar Wood, or Minett, but rarely if ever can they do it with the same kind of style and grace as a woody.

Writing this book has been like an unexpected trip back to those times in my childhood. As I researched the history of each boat, examined each photograph, I was reminded of those moments on the dock at Campbell's Landing, wondering what kind of wonderful craft would usher us back to the cottage. And, of course, I was reminded of my grandad, who taught me my love of boats, and whose legacy has provided me with a wealth of information and documentation regarding these spectacular vessels.

Each one of these boats is so special and unique. Those that have survived to the turn of this century have been able to do so because of the loving care of someone, perhaps many people, who recognized and appreciated their beauty and charm from right from the start, and was willing to give the extra care needed to ensure that their boat would continue to skim the waters in the new millennium. It is my hope that this book will provide those people with a trip down their own memory lane, and will give those who haven't had the pleasure of owning, driving, or riding in these magical vessels a taste of what has become for many of us a pleasant addiction.

James W. Ogilvie Knowles

May 1999

The wooden motorboat was as much a part of the American Dream during the early part of this century as were the two-car garage and the backyard barbecue. From small inland lakes to coastal communities, the wooden boat has served as workhorse, taxi, pleasure craft, and status symbol. Naturally, the development over time of the "woody" (as they are sometimes affectionately known) has resulted in a wide variety of forms and styles; the term can as easily apply to a small runabout as to a 60-foot (18.3m) luxury sedan cruiser. At heart, though, all woodies share the same essential features—beautiful, flowing lines, exotic hardwoods, and a demand for care and attention that, if met, results in a vessel that can outlast its owner.

The arrival of the industrial age saw many major advances in the fields of engineering and technology. By the early 1900s, this progress was being applied to marine vessels, their engines, and their equipment. Innovations such as the use of a carburetor to drastically improve engine performance and the harnessing of electricity to replace naphtha gas changed motorboating from a slow and sometimes dangerous affair into an activity that could be enjoyed by the whole family. As the economy boomed and life's luxuries became more attainable, the woody developed alongside the automobile as both practical necessity and status symbol. Not surprisingly, developments in the marine and automobile industries often paralleled one another—as the car improved so did the motorboat. Companies such as Cummins, Universal, Eveready, and Evinrude took advantage of the improvements that were being made in engine technology, adapted those improvements for the rigorous demands of marine use, and thus helped shape the foundation of the marine engine industry.

In the period before the First World War, the boat builders and designers of North America worked at installing these new and improved inventions in watercraft whose hull lines were changing as fast as the times. The lakes, oceans, and rivers of North America now featured all sorts of uncommon craft being tested—some successfully and some unsuccessfully. The time was marked by a great deal of experimentation and exploration. What would work? What would not? Was it better to have the engine amidships or at the stern? How fast can we get this boat to go? Why is it so darn noisy? There were many questions and only one way to find the answers—design it, build it, and try it out.

War inevitably leads to many improvements in technology, and the effect of World War I on the motorboat was no exception. Important gains were made in boat-building practices when many of the larger companies (such as Chris-Craft, Higgins, Greavette, and Wheeler) honed their techniques by supplying landing craft, attack boats, and patrol boats to the effort to quash the Hun. These military applications had long-term repercussions in that they not only improved the product but also provided a surplus of engines and parts once the war was over. This lowered prices, increased availability, and made it easier for middle-class Americans to own a motorboat. This greater

OPPOSITE: The luxurious upholstery and exotic hardwoods that are the hallmarks of 1950s boat design require rigorous, tender, and loving care. Perfectly maintained vessels like this Greavette are a testament not only to the quality of the boatbuilders, but to the dedication of the owners of these boats.

11

ease of access to motorboats is reflected in the advertising of the time. In fact, it is during this period that boating advertising really began to take off, in magazines such as *Motor Boating* and the *Rudder*, as the industry began to realize that it had a growing, eager market. The following excerpt, from a Chris-Craft ad of the thirties, captures the image that wooden boat manufacturers had created:

> *Every family is entitled to at least know the delight of Chris-Craft riding, its usefulness—its joy-bringing and health-building properties. Let the tired businessman lengthen his life and give happiness to the whole family by providing them with the multitude of clean thrills and joys available only through Chris-Craft ownership. . . . Chris-Crafting is recreation in itself. It recreates those who use it both in body and in mind.*

The push was on to get as many people as possible into a boat, and the public obeyed by making the boating industry one of the largest growth industries of the twenties and thirties.

At the onset of World War II, with the industry still alive after the Great Depression, business continued to boom. The sales of runabouts and cruisers during the forties surpassed those of even the late twenties, a time that had seen great successes for boat builders and sellers. The Second World War placed even greater demands on the industry, demands that were met and exceeded. In the United States, large companies such as Wheeler, Higgins, and Chris-Craft again received orders and quotas from the Navy that pushed their production facilities to the limit. The vessels that the military and defense forces needed ranged from 36-foot (11m) landing craft to minesweepers, with orders for 400 to 1000 boats coming in at one time. These manufacturers and others were able to increase their production level and pump out thousands of vessels to aid in the conflict.

The fifties saw the boat business grow with a vengeance. There were so many new innovations that it is difficult to keep track of who was doing what. There were the Canadian builders of the Muskokas. Greavette, Minette, Shields, and Duke were still filling custom orders and producing one-of-a-kind "runabout" models. At the same time, the large American yards were mass-producing cruisers. In general, however, the decade was characterized by highly stylized designs and the same kind of zeal for streamlining that was all the rage in the automobile industry. This kind of design excess was made possible by the advent of quality plywood and glass-reinforced plastic. The flexibility, malleability, and relative affordability of these materials meant that the average consumer could now purchase vessels that were often works of art. The downside, of course, was that the availability of these cheaper materials coincided with (or led to, depending on one's point of view) an increase in the cost of quality wood. Thus, for the first time, building quality wooden boats in the traditional style was becoming reserved for those who had the means to support the old style of craftsmanship.

As marine-grade plywood and fiberglass made their presence more strongly felt in the boating world, builders strove to decide if and how these new production materials should be incorporated into their boats. After all, using some fiberglass to create a fin on the deck of what was basically a wooden boat was one thing, but making an entire boat out of this new material was quite another. Builders worried that unproven materials such as these were a very big risk and might not stand up over time. As anyone who has had experience with some of the earliest fiberglass boats will attest, these worries were not completely unfounded. However, improvements in these newer areas of the industry quickly made these products indispensable; strength, lightness, reliability, and greater design freedom eventually led almost all the major manufacturers to turn to plastic. Building boats out of wood the old-fashioned way became even more the province of enthusiasts and purists; only a few companies such as Duke and Greavette of Muskoka ignored the advances and continued to build with hardwood and cloth.

BELOW: *Jessica,* a seventy-five-year-old wooden commuter, provides transportation on the waters around Miami, Florida.

PADDLE TO POWER

⊸⊶⊷

THE ARRIVAL OF THE INBOARD ENGINE

The Muskoka Lakes were undoubtedly among the most important contributors to the early development of the woody. Although wooden motorboats were also developed in many parts of the United States and in other places in North America (and, indeed, the world), these three major Canadian inland lakes located approximately one hundred miles (160km) north of Toronto were very appealing to boaters and attracted many of the early inventors and experimenters. Foremost among their attractive qualities were the relative calmness of the lakes, the somewhat easier winters compared to the Great Lakes and other seaside moorings, and, of course, the stunning beauty of the area.

These three lakes—Lake Muskoka, Lake Rousseau, and Lake Joseph, along with the several hundred smaller lakes that make up the region—began to attract tourists from the south, including many wealthy American tourists who were interested in investment close to home but still wanted property that was remote and natural enough to make them feel like they were "getting away from it all." Sprinkled with thousands of islands and beautiful bays sheltered from the north winds, the Muskoka Lakes almost seem to have been made to order for recreational boating. At the time, the private beaches and coves called out for lodges and estates to be built. Many locals as well as visitors from the United States were only too happy to heed that call and carve out a little place (or a massive resort) on these wonderful shores.

The people who ventured north in the late 1800s were more than tourists—they were adventurers, pioneers in a way. After all, the Muskoka Lakes region was largely unexplored and totally undeveloped at the time. Armed with maps and rough charts of the lakes, they set

OPPOSITE: The booming resort community around the Muskoka Lakes meant that there were—and are—plenty of wealthy residents needing practical but stylish transportation. Commuters like *Mavourneen* get folks across from island to island and cottage to cottage.

out to build the haunts of the rich and famous. Coming from Cleveland, Buffalo, Pittsburgh, Toronto, and elsewhere, these wealthy businessmen and land barons staked their claim to the north and in doing so greatly influenced the development of the classic runabout as we know it today.

Since the region generally lacked the roads necessary to transport equipment and materials to the more inaccessible parts of the lakes, craftsmen in the area began filling the orders for working boats. Hiring local builders to supply these boats made a great deal of sense—since the cost of trucking the boats was quite high, and what roads did exist tended to be unreliable most of the time, it was a much better option for the buyer to have the boat built on the scene by locals rather than trucking it from the States or Toronto. With the opening of the locks at Port Carling in 1871, access became available by water to and from Lake Muskoka (the southernmost lake) to Rosseau and Joseph (to the north), making it much easier for the local folk to ply their trade. Such trade included setting and tending trap lines when the lakes were frozen and, during the spring thaw, moving the furs that were produced by those trap lines down to market in Gravenhurst, the most southerly town at the foot of Lake Muskoka.

Personally, Jim remembers about thirty years ago going up to Campbell's Landing on the southwestern shore of Lake Muskoka to get over to his grandfather's boathouse on Browning Island in order to check on it. His mother was later horrified to learn from him that when he walked into Campbell's Landing he found the large works building packed full of dead animals all at different stages of the fur-processing treatment. This was a common sight around the lakes throughout their history. In the summer, boat builders would build and repair boats and in the winter those same shops and buildings would be used for storage, as skinning houses, and also (if they weren't being used for anything else) for the building of personal watercraft. This is one of the reasons we see so many single-design and one-off models in the Muskokas. This tendency was certainly only enhanced by the availability of do-it-yourself books such as the 1930 edition of Modern Mechanix' *How to Build Twenty Boats*. Such books were must-reads at the time for anyone living on an isolated waterfront.

Further to the south, on and around the Great Lakes, development of the woody was also moving along. The situation was similar: residents of the area needed a reliable means of getting around on the water. The lay of the land—cliffs jutting out into the bays and swamps dividing lush acres of wildflowers—meant that the ancient and stony face of the Canadian Shield presented itself just about everywhere.

Finding good and reliable transportation around the Lakes in those days was a necessary but not an easy task. As in the Muskokas, the more isolated areas of the Lakes had virtually no roads. Any roads that did exist were usually impassable except during the summer months. The financial cost alone of driving even the most rudimentary of roads through the forest and rock was prohibitive, not to mention the cost in effort and exertion. Until this point, access to many of these areas was open only to those who had the gumption to paddle and portage canoes or the fortitude to endure the noise and smoke on one of the steamers that plied those waters. Of course, transportation by water was the best way to get around in the very rocky and somewhat swampy areas of both the Great Lakes and the Muskokas. It is not surprising that wooden motorboats were developed over time to meet that need.

When settlers first came into these areas, the only existing means of water transport was the dugout and bark canoe. Built and perfected by the First Nations residents, these stable craft were well suited to travel on the lakes. The personal canoes of an Indian family were light, maneuverable, and easy to handle, with the ability to carry large loads with little problem. For bigger jobs such as those involving the fur trade, there were larger cargo canoes that did the job well but were very heavy to portage over rough water and waterfalls.

Even though the Peterborough Canoe Company did not invent the canoe, they were certainly instrumental in the development of the modern version. In 1879 the Ontario Canoe Company (Peterborough's original name) was organized to build the first board canoes. At

OPPOSITE: Dating from the early days of the twentieth century, this meticulously restored gas-engine launch was great for speeding around on lakes and rivers. Mounted in the middle of the vessel, the flywheel for this little 4-horsepower engine was something to avoid when cranking her over by hand.

ABOVE: An identification plate from an 1898 steam launch. Around the turn of the century, steam launches were a popular means of transportation around inland lakes.

17

RIGHT: The *Ellen* is a Fay & Bowen design that lies somewhere between a simple vessel and a floating sculpture.

European exhibitions in 1883, 1885, 1886, 1900, and 1901, Peterborough Canoes won gold medals, demonstrating that their excellence had given them worldwide acclaim.

Although other types of vessels were being rowed and powered around the Muskoka Lakes (the majority having been initially brought up from the States), one of the first serious attempts in the region to move from dugouts and canoes to a different type of craft was estimated to have begun about 1868. Around that time in Port Carling, W. J. Johnston decided to build himself a rowboat. This little boat turned out to be a great success for him and his family. As the tourist industry approached cottage country he continued to build these small craft for rent and eventually became one of the premier builders of launches in the area. His rowboats were such a success that he and his family set up two liveries, and produced more than three hundred rowboats for rent on the lakes in 1870.

The reciprocating steam engine was the only reliable mechanical means of transport from the mid-1800s to the 1890s. Large steam-fitted ferries were used to transport people in the major waterfront cities on the lakes, oceans, and rivers of North America. The steam launches being built for the rich were long and beamy, big enough to carry the huge steam engine required to propel the vessel and as many passengers as that particular jaunt called for. The smaller steam launches of the period, however, were often quaint little open craft that were well suited to the nattily uniformed captain and the frilly dresses worn by women in the first decade of the twentieth century. The personal steam launch did not stay around for long, however, because just as this means of transportation was being perfected, the gasoline engine made its debut. The comparatively easy operation of this new invention and the requirement that steamboat operators have a valid steam engineer's license were major contributing factors to the demise of the steam launch.

18

Gas engine launches were being built in the early 1900s in the States and in Canada but, at least initially, they were often unreliable and ungainly. This was soon to change. The end of the First World War brought about a glut of engines on the market, which satisfied the needs of builders who were now experimenting with all types of engines and hull configurations to see who could get the fastest, driest, and most comfortable ride. The open-hulled rowboats of the time were perfect for the mechanically inclined entrepreneur boatbuilder to experiment with. The next twenty years saw the rapid development of a gas engine that was smaller in size but with more horsepower and much more reliability. These efforts paid off, allowing builders like Johnston, Gar Wood, Ditchburn, Chris-Craft, Greavette, and Minett to incorporate such engines into their product.

Around 1905, one of the first engines for a smaller boat to undergo experimentation was the Waterman 2-horsepower engine and the Waterman "porto motor." The Waterman Motor Company of Detroit was producing an outboard motor and a 2-horsepower flywheel inboard model that was quite efficient due to weight reduction and advancements in engine design and construction. At the same time, W. J. Johnston applied for and received a patent on a contraption that he called a "propulsion device for boats." Dubbed a "dispro" (short for "disappearing propeller"), this package allowed a skiff or canoe to be built with an inboard motor and an articulating propeller shaft that would hide up in the hull in shallow water and, if struck by an underwater object, would deflect up inside the hull without damage. While there were other launches on the lake that were using much larger engines, a big engine required a longer, wider, and deeper boat. That was all very well for mucking about in deep water, but Mr. Johnston's dispro with its shallow draft could be taken into waters that most motorboats wouldn't dare enter. It was affordable, fairly reliable, and quickly proved itself not only a great touring craft but also a real workhorse.

Very plain in the beginning, the 16-foot (4.9m) double-ended lapstrake hull of the dispro with ribs of white oak and bench seats of cedar looked very much like a wide canoe. Like the canoe, these sturdy vessels could carry large loads. The inside front cover of *The Greatest Little Motor Boat Afloat* (cowritten by William G. Ogilvie, Jim's grandfather) features a photograph of a dispro loaded with seventeen men with plenty of freeboard still showing. As recorded in *The Greatest Little Motorboat Afloat* and in his own book, *Way, Way Down North*, Ogilvie started and completed a 1500-mile (2413.5km) surveying journey from Edmonton to Fort Norman in a 16-foot (4.9m) dispro that towed a 16-foot (4.9m) Peterborough canoe and an 18-foot (5.5m) Chestnut freight canoe. As Grandpa Boo himself put it in *Way, Way Down North*:

In addition to the aforementioned food list we figured that we would need to carry eighty-four gallons of gasoline with the necessary oil for mix and that a further supply of fifty gallons of gas would be shipped by riverboat direct to our destination. Our Disappearing Propeller's little 3hp engine averaged approximately 25 miles [40km] to the gallon. That was a foremost reason for the choosing of this craft. Other reasons were that it was sturdily built and with its double end design it would be a good sea boat—these sea going qualities enhanced by the disappearing propeller being located just aft of amidships and always in the water regardless how rough the sea. Then, of course, the fact that the propeller could be raised into the safety of the propeller housing enabling the boat to be hauled out on shore was another factor in its favour. Last, but not least there were many hundreds in use and they had gained a reputation for dependability far in excess of the outboard motors which were just beginning to come on the market. These were bulky, very hard to start and not nearly so light on gas consumption.

These tough little boats were to be built for the next forty years, with two plants in operation, in North Tonawanda, New York, and in the original factory in Port Carling. Ogilvie acted as sales representative and eventually moved up to general manager of the company, so it is perhaps not too surprising that he sung the praises of the "dippy" (as it affectionately came to be known). He had good reason, though. With over a thousand dippies being built over forty years of business, the boat had earned its reputation. The company was operated by different owners at different times; Greavette Boat Works owned it in the end. Ironically, the demise of the dispro began with improvements to the very gas engine that provided its power. As technology advanced, there arrived on the market a new product whose speed, reliability, and power would eventually edge these trustworthy but slow little boats into retirement—the outboard engine.

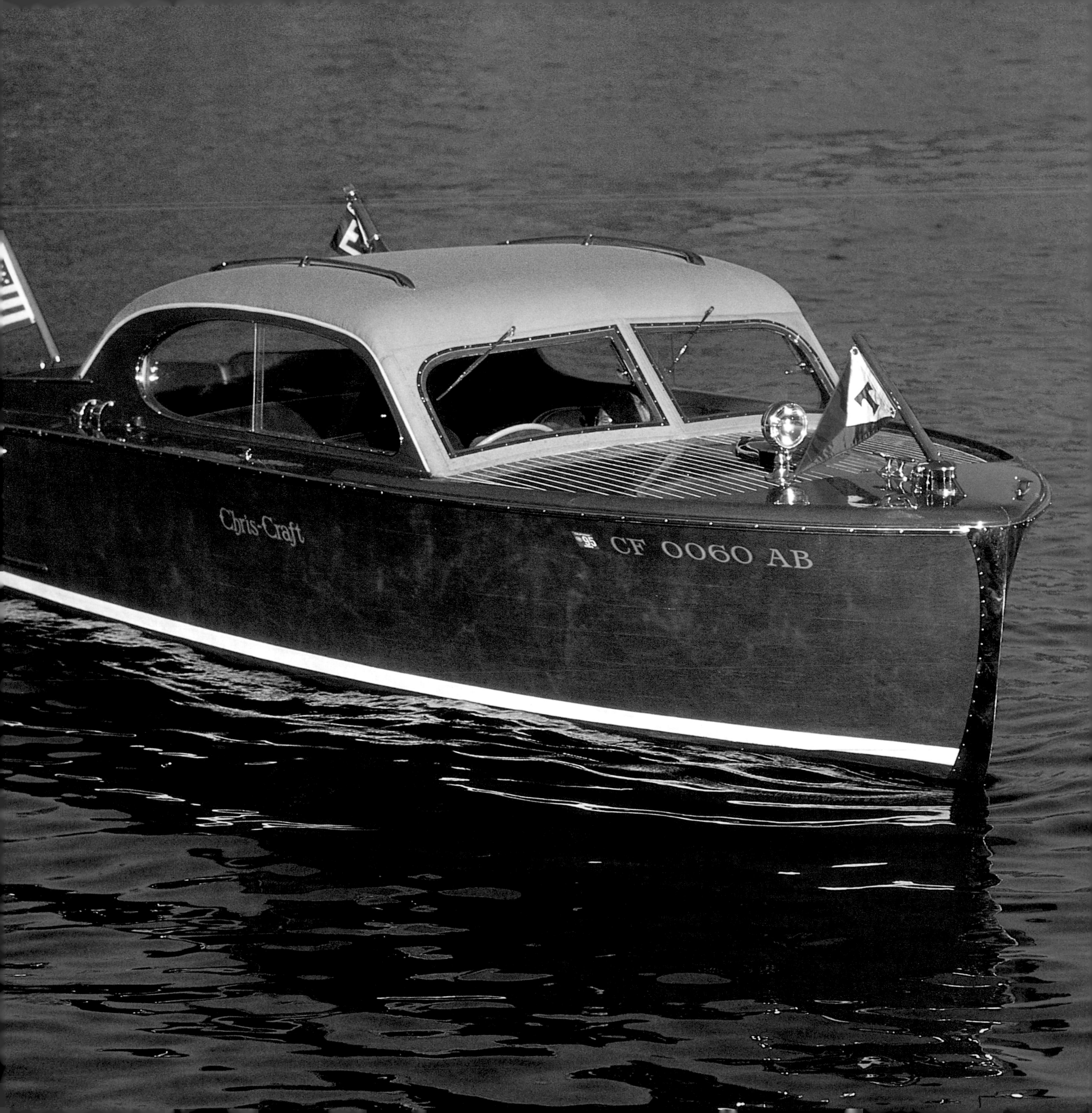
Chris-Craft
CF 0060 AB

UTILITIES

◁~◁~▷

THE WOODY GOES TO WORK

The progress of the runabout now took off in two different directions. With the development of a reliable outboard by Elto, Johnston, and other up-and-comers, the smaller craft that were being used for getting into shallows and going up rivers could now provide the fisherman or the hunter access to new areas more rapidly and more efficiently. The new "rowboat" motors, as they were called, would tilt up automatically and they were much faster than the slower 2- and 3-horsepower inboard engines being used. Easier to store, usually easier to start, and with the added benefit of being portable, these outboard motors could be put on almost any dingy or rowboat. The result was a craft that was much more maneuverable than an inboard and could be made ready for action at a moment's notice. The other important consideration was price—having an outboard engine meant that you could add a motor to an existing boat and not have to purchase another vessel if you wanted a change. There is no question that the outboard motor was a major contributing factor in the boating boom, putting the sport within reach of almost everyone's pocketbook.

Engineering histories reveal that a Frenchman named DeSanderai conceived of the idea in 1876. Unfortunately, since it was a steam-driven engine, the vessel and its power plant spent most of the time on the bottom. In 1893 American piano tycoon William Steinway exhibited an outboard motor built by Gottlieb Daimler (a German car manufacturer) at the Chicago World's Fair. Steinway actually built one hundred of the motors and found something of an early market for them. However, the venture was not profitable enough and so was dropped.

OPPOSITE: The influence of contemporary automotive design is unmistakable in this Chris-Craft sedan. Fitted with a custom top, all it needs is a spare tire and some running boards.

23

These first outboards were mostly failures, and the issue of who first produced a viable outboard is up for debate. The Outboard Marine Corporation would probably credit the invention of the first successful outboard to one Ole Evinrude, a Norwegian immigrant who settled in Dane County, Wisconsin. On the other hand, the Kiekhaefer Corporation would undoubtedly claim that the inventor was Cameron B. Waterman, a young Yale law student. In fact, both contributed greatly, though Waterman was slightly ahead of Evinrude and was the man who actually coined the term *outboard motor*. He tried but was unable to copyright the term because of its generic origin. Evinrude, on the other hand, had the advantage of being married to a shrewd and clever woman who was able to turn the talents of this shy engineering genius into cold, hard capital.

During the first years of the 1900s, Waterman lived at Spruce Harbor on Lake Superior and studied law. His first crude effort to eliminate rowing was to mount an air-cooled bicycle engine onto the stern of his fishing boat. He theorized that if the chain could drive a wheel, it could also drive a propeller. The idea worked fairly well, but the chain kept falling off the bottom sprocket and so in 1905 he gave up on the idea. At that point, Waterman and his friend George Thrall developed a driveshaft and bevel gear arrangement that worked well. This new development was quickly worked into a prototype and in 1906 commercial production of the Waterman Porto Motor began. In the first year, twenty-five motors were built. In each of the next two years, a total of three thousand motors were built and sold. By 1909, when Evinrude marketed his

BELOW: Small, open vessels like the *Ol' Smoothie* helped bridge the transition from manually powered canoes to motorized launches. More stable than a canoe, and with a four-horse engine amidships, they had a shallow draft that allowed access to waters along the shore.

NC 2257 CF

first engine, Waterman had sold six thousand units. Waterman's career in the business ended in 1916, when he sold his interests to the Arrow Motor and Marine Co. of New York. Not until 1955 was he given the recognition he deserved, with a presentation and ceremony at the New York Boat Show. He died a year later at the age of seventy-three, a successful lawyer.

Despite Waterman's earlier start, the man with the greatest vision and determination was Ole Evinrude. In April 1909, Evinrude's first

outboard was tested on the Kinnickinnic River in Wisconsin. The orders trickled in at first but then began to snowball. With his new wife's accounting and financial savvy and Evinrude's mechanical skills, the tiny firm soon turned into a small giant, with the slogan "No rowing— just going." In 1921 Evinrude stormed the market with a new outboard, the Elto, which stood for "Evinrude Light Twin Outboard." Tens of thousands were sold. In 1928 Elto brought out the first four-cylinder motor to great acclaim. The Evinrude firm merged with the Lockwood Motor Company in 1929 and formed the Outboard Marine Corporation. In 1936 this successful company bought out the Johnson Motor Company and continued production of the Johnson, Elto, and Evinrude lines.

Of course, the influence and desires of the wealthy continued to be felt throughout this period. The rich demanded the best and most beautiful boats for their recreation and utility, a demand that produced some very beautiful designs. Combining different types of hardwoods, extensive use of chrome, sumptuous upholstery, and the latest in electronic gadgetry, the boat builders who were lucky enough to provide for the most exclusive clientele had an opportunity to push their skills to the limit. Naturally, these flashy vessels had to have the very latest in power and thus served as a valuable proving ground for the latest improvements in engine technology. These recreational runabouts weren't simply skiffs or lake utilities anymore. They were becoming works of art—something to show off and be seen in.

ABOVE: A pair of 1930s Electri-crafts moored in the shallows.

25

ABOVE: The vibrant splash of metal against wood gives a unique spirit to the controls of classic powerboats. The engine controls of a classic Elco cruiser, top, put those on a fiberglass boat to shame. The cockpit of *Little Miss Maple Leaf*, bottom, a 1934 18-foot (5.5m) Greavette designed by Hacker, is more than a helm, it's a piece of history.

RIGHT: Utility craft like this 1950 Hutchinson may not have been the most elegant of vessels on the lake, but they certainly got the job done.

In the Muskokas, the building of boats was on a smaller, more personal level. Boats were made to order or built by the owner for his own use. In the States, however, the major companies were gearing up for mass production. Some of these companies, shortly to become famous names in America's boating history, were getting together for the general improvement of their product. With a builder like Chris Smith teaming up with the money and competitive spirit of Gar Wood along with the design genius of John L. Hacker, it was only a matter of time until the runabout reached production levels that almost equaled that of the automobile.

Once the marine engine became more reliable, a variety of motorized vessels were developed that could take advantage of the new power and assist in the work of daily life. Chris-Craft, Greavette, Gar Wood, Johnston, and Barnes were just a few of the names producing craft that can be loosely grouped together under the name *utilities*. They were advertised and sold as runabouts at the time, but today a distinction can be made by looking at the plainness of the design and the functions these less expensive models performed. There were no paneled cockpits, the seats had little padding, and the boats had few extra toys. These vessels were generally rough and ready, used to ferry freight, supplies, and people to locations that were difficult or impossible to reach by land. Utilities were particularly indispensable for those developing recreational properties on lakefronts and islands. Because a significant portion of this period of development falls within the Great Depression, much of the innovation in utility design was again financially fueled by the needs of the wealthiest families. It is also noteworthy that, as the industry became more established, many related companies were formed to meet the needs of the motorized boating community. Advertising by Cummins, Universal, and other companies began to appear in popular magazines.

As the inboard gas engine was developing, the larger boat liveries of the southern United States were thriving. Names such as Chris-Craft, Hackercraft, and Gar Wood were producing launches at the high end of the market for pleasure use and utilities at the lower end of the market for those who did not have the financial wherewithal or for those who needed a good sturdy work boat. These large companies were also producing smaller boats that could be fitted with the latest outboard motors. As mentioned, in Muskoka companies such as Duke, Ditchburn, and Minett were also doing well but were still concentrating on individual orders. They left the work of mass production to their larger cousins south of the border.

BELOW: Although the open-deck is the trademark of a true utility, many sailors prefer the versatility of a closed deck, which allows them to get about their chores in inclement weather.

The utilities were the workhorses, often seen moving people and goods between the cottages and lodges of the lakes. Chris-Craft was one of the major builders of these smaller working-class boats, which generally featured an open design with the engine amidships. Mr. Chris Smith, the founder of the company, forged ahead in the thirties and went into mass production of these models as well as a number of other design styles (most notably the more expensive recreational runabouts). Utilities were usually displacement-style boats designed to transport people and luggage and, when not working, to provide enough roominess for fishing or touring. In a 1939 sales brochure, Chris-Craft claimed, "They are big, roomy, all-purpose boats, ideally planned for fishing, yet so comfortable and beautiful in appearance and styling that they fit right into the scheme of things for cruising, for bathing, for general utility use and for commuting."

The typical Chris-Craft utility was built mainly from two types of wood. The main frames, keel, and battens were all made of mahogany, while the bottom frames and chines were white oak. They arrived from the factory with standard equipment, including an automatic bailer, combination cushion–life preservers, electric navigation lights, a horn, and a choice of instrument packages. The three-unit package of instruments included an ammeter, oil gauge, and tachometer. The other packages supplemented these with a temperature gauge, a gasoline gauge, and a clock. Equipped with 40- to 105-horsepower Chryslers or Gray Marine engines, these craft could reach speeds of 12 to 30 mph (19–48kph). At a cost of approximately $1900, these boats quickly became production-line items. The Chris-Craft plant at Algonac, Michigan, produced only four of these boats in 1922; by 1929 the numbers had increased to almost a thousand.

Gar Wood, very successful at this time in the racing industry, decided to listen to the public demand for boats that could serve double duty as both utility and pleasure craft. Accordingly, he opened his plant in Marysville, Michigan, in 1930, with facilities capable of producing motorboats for customers who wanted the very best. This plant could produce more than twelve hundred boats a year and still maintain Wood's

ABOVE: This 1931–32 Electri-craft 18-foot (5.5m) boat was clean and quiet, and well ahead of its time.

very high standards of quality. In 1935 Gar Wood offered its first utility to the boat-hungry public, a 20-foot (6.1m) model. In 1936, with the popularity of the 1935 model proven, the plant produced two utilities, an 18-foot (5.5m) and a 20-foot (6.1m) model. In 1937 Gar Wood introduced a 24-foot (7.3m) utility that was so popular it remained in active production until 1942. The company improved on existing utility designs in 1939, adding a sedan top and enclosing the majority of the vessel. The combination of a cabin with the proven utility hull, known as an "overnighter," was a big hit in the industry. This represents some of the first steps toward the modern cabin cruiser as we know it today.

Chris-Craft introduced their "newest Utility" to the market in 1932, but in fact this "new" utility was just a stripped-down 24-foot (7.3m) runabout. Gone were the extra seats; now, with only one driver's seat, it was advertised as being "particularly well adapted for fishing, cargo carrying, and harbor work." The reason for this stripped-down model was that the Depression was now starting to bite at their books and Chris-Craft had to produce a model affordable to the average person who hadn't been destroyed by the Crash. There were a multitude of others building utilities at this time but the Depression filtered out the small-time builders and left the public, for better or worse, with products from the larger outfits.

OPPOSITE: This 1910 Perkins one-off launch served as part utility, part commuter; the large, open cockpit provided enough useful room to transport passengers, but was just as often used to carry building materials, groceries, or other supplies.

LEFT: *Molly-O*, a 1930 Chris-Craft deluxe utility, blends rugged functionality with a clean, slick profile. The pleasing, crisp lines of the 24³/₄ foot (7.5m) vessel reflect the classic styling of the 1930s.

COMMUTERS AND LAUNCHES

—❦—

GETTING THERE

Naturally, once recreational properties were developed on lakefronts, islands, riverfronts, and remote coastal communities, a need arose for vessels that could ferry people from home and work to "the cottage" and to private resorts with grace and comfort. More than ever before, attention was paid to ensuring that the passenger had as pleasant a traveling experience as possible. Interiors transformed from often spartan quarters with hard wooden benches to more luxurious environments with padded seats and the beginnings of amenities. At the same time, sightseeing by water was becoming more popular. To fulfill all these needs, companies such as Huckins, Greavette, Ditchburn, Gar Wood, and Chris-Craft continued to produce commuters and launches that combined comfort with efficiency.

Throughout the rise of the utility, the launch had continued its climb to popularity. Once your lakeside lodge or cottage was built, you needed to have a way to get out on the water for sightseeing, visiting the neighbors, or socializing with friends at the lodge across the lake. To accommodate their guests' commuters and runabouts, the owners of these ritzy "cabins" built boat liveries on their properties, which were situated in prime locations. Private lodges and estates such as Windemere House and Clevelands House on Lake Rosseau were just a few of the elegant outposts in the north. As seen in *The Greatest Little Motor Boat Afloat*, pictures of Windemere House and Elgin House show a bustle of boating activity, from rentals to sightseeing tours. The smaller and more humble utility boats served a purpose even in these luxurious settings, generally as rental units for guests who did not bring a boat of their own. The real prestige, however, lay in arriving in

OPPOSITE: The gleaming wood and mirror-like chrome of *Miss Lindy* attests to a great deal of meticulous care from the loving owner of this classic Ditchburn.

33

BELOW: The Muskoka Lakes boasted many classic designs and witnessed a variety of styles over the years. Commuters and launches provided easy and stylish transportation across the lakes.

your own elegant launch or commuter with a paid driver at the helm ready to pick up guests from the local ferry dock or take passengers on sightseeing trips around the lake.

The builders of these fine pieces of history were from the Muskoka area as well as from south of the line. The big companies such as Chris-Craft and Gar Wood were still the leaders in the United States at this time. Gar Wood, whose runabouts are today some of the most sought-after woodies, had established a reputation as a producer of some of the highest-quality launches and commuters. The eagerness with which present-day collectors and enthusiasts pursue these classic boats is a testament to the durability and timelessness of the company's product.

Garfield Arthur Wood had been raised around boats. His father was a ferryboat captain, so much of his time as a boy and then as a young man was spent on and near the water. Something of a mechanical genius, Wood established his empire by inventing the hydraulic lift. As his fortune grew manufacturing this necessary and invaluable item, so did his other passion—the desire to become seriously involved in a hobby he loved, speedboat racing.

In 1916 two giants in the industry teamed up when Wood bought the Chris Smith boat works in Algonac, Michigan. They had a purpose—to design and build a boat that was faster than any other. With Gar Wood designing and Chris Smith building, their talents

BELOW: A 1921 Gar Wood hangs just off the reeds at the end of another beautiful day on the lake.

RIGHT: *Lizzy*, a 20½ foot (6.2m) 1939 Gar Wood sedan, bobs dockside in the Thousand Islands, at the mouth of the St. Lawrence River in Ontario.

BELOW: Triple cockpit designs like this 1929 26-foot (7.9m) Chris-Craft runabout provide pilot and passengers with a smooth, comfortable, stylish ride.

OPPOSITE: With bow lines leading fore and aft for easy landing, *Kartozian*, a 1915 Hutchinson, was probably originally operated by a uniformed captain.

complemented each other well; together they made boat-racing history by winning five straight Gold Cups and two Harmsworth Trophies in 1920 and 1921.

Just when it seemed that Wood and Smith together were unbeatable, in 1922 the rules governing the Gold Cup races were changed. The committee on racing wanted to include more gentleman racers and, to Wood's dismay at the time, if he was to conform to their rules he would have to produce a different type of boat than the ones he had been producing. Little did anyone know that these changes would cause a boom in the runabout business and rocket both Gar Wood and later Chris-Craft to the top with the production of a fast gentleman racer.

By 1924, Gar Wood's "Baby Gar" had made its mark on society's wealthy. It was a safe, comfortable triple cockpit that could outperform almost anything on the water. Dignitaries like William Randolph Hearst, John Dodge, and P. K. Wrigley bought and flaunted these gentleman racers, soon making them *the* boat to own among the very well-to-do.

Chris Smith, meanwhile, decided to get back into business for himself and in 1922 left Gar Wood and started Chris-Craft Boats. To reduce the cost and make the boats more available to

ABOVE: The luxury commuters of the 1920s were used to transport wealthy businessmen from their summer cottages to their offices in nearby cities.

the public, Smith wanted to go into a production-line style of building. While a major part of the early Chris-Craft line consisted of smaller runabouts and utilities, Smith also introduced a line of commuter models. As the First World War ended, the age of the pleasure boat came into its own, with tested engines and new electronics aboard that allowed the public to explore this strange new thing called "leisure" in an exciting and fashionable way. After all, this was the Roaring Twenties, and gallivanting about in boats was becoming as popular with the urban flappers and hangers-on as it was it was among the quieter lakefront resorts of the rich and powerful. In New York Harbor and on the waters

LEFT: The very narrow beam and canoe-like shape of *Pausar*, an early Ditchburn, betray its age, while the coverable cockpit suggests its use as a commuter.

of the Detroit River, it was fashionable to commute to work at speeds of up to 50 mph (80kph) by commuter yacht. Similarly, it was all the rage in Chicago to tour Lake Michigan by water taxi and return at the end of the day to the Chicago Navy Pier or to the Edgewater Beach Hotel.

Between 1928 and 1931, Chris-Craft produced sixty-five 38-foot (11.6m) and 30-foot (9.1m) commuters to carry the new breed of businessman to work. Their cruiser was one of the first to be equipped not only with a 200-horsepower engine but also a toilet, curtains, and roll-down windows. Of the 1929 30-foot (9.1m) Custom Commuter, the Smiths would say:

LEFT: The *Cat's Pjs* is a Chris-Craft flat-deck built around 1929. The flat-deck model was built in 24 and 26-foot (7.3 and 7.9m) lengths.

ABOVE: The steering deck from an early flush-deck commuter.

ABOVE: Chris-Craft proudly emblazoned their name on all their poducts, from their grandest cruisers right down to the humblest cleat, as on this 1929 model.

OPPOSITE: Touring boats like this gem were particularly popular in the early 1900s. Cocktails, anyone?

In the first year of production many men of great prominence sought to buy this remarkable new craft; a few who placed late orders were disappointed in not being able to secure one. The demand exceeded our expectations because so many had been waiting for just such a craft. A busy year has now put us in position to supply a larger number of these weather-closed, twelve passenger, drawing room commuters. . . . Here is, in truth, a travelling home, where one may comfortably pass the time between office and home. Seclusion, reading writing or games, luncheon or business meeting are available to every owner of a Chris-Craft Commuter.

Commuters tended to grow in size and comfort until 1934, when Chris-Craft released their 48-foot (14.6m) taxi commuter, which could accommodate up to sixty passengers. The other major builders of the time were also producing larger commuters and taxis, as well as keeping a mainstay of smaller boats for smaller budgets. This latter line would be emphasized more heavily when the Depression hit, but until then the twenties were a boom time for the builders of wooden runabouts and other craft. If one looks at the numbers of pleasure motorboats in operation just before the bubble burst, it is clear that America had taken to the water in a big way:

TOTAL NUMBER OF PLEASURE MOTORBOATS IN OPERATION IN 1929

(from "Boating Business," January 1930)

Documented Motorboats	2,910
Numbered Motorboats	236,514
Unnumbered Motorboats	708,000
Outboard Motorboats	350,000
Total	*1,297,424*

Another company of great significance in the Muskokas during these early years was Ditchburn, one of the area's most reputable builders of launches, day cruisers, and runabouts. The Ditchburn family's marine history goes back many centuries and they made many notable contributions in the field of marine technology, including giving Britain her first ironclad battleship. From the late 1800s to their closing in 1938, Ditchburn built many, many boats, from canoes and rowboats to 120-foot (36.6m) cruisers.

RIGHT: The Fred Adams launch *Lazy Lady* offers the fun of an open-air cabin with the protection of a convertible cover.

BELOW: The *Wild Goose*, despite its sleek, streamlined profile, still leaves plenty of room for passengers.

LEFT: An excellent example of an early commuter, this 1925 Fay & Bowen features a low profile and a covered cockpit for shelter during foul weather.

The H. Ditchburn Boat Manufacturing Co., Ltd., was started by Henry Ditchburn in 1893, although it was not a major concern until the early 1900s, when Henry's nephew Herbert took over the operation in Gravenhurst. Uncle Henry died in 1912 but was noted as being the first man to build a gasoline-powered launch in Muskoka. By 1921, building canoes and dinghies was a thing of the past for Ditchburn; the orders for commuters and launches were becoming the mainstay of the business.

The first big boat out of the Ditchburn yard was the *Kawandag II*, a 73-foot (22.3m) displacement cruiser. Powered by twin eight-cylinder Sterlings, she could reach speeds of 24 mph (38.6kph). Recognizable as most Ditchburns were by the almost vertical stem and knife-sharp bow, the *Kawandag II* widened to a beam of 12 feet (3.7m). It was a work of art, with an enclosed wheelhouse forward, open air seating amidships, and enclosed seating aft. This vessel was most likely designed by Bert Hawker, who had left Minett two years before and began

designing for Ditchburn in 1919, remaining with them until 1930. This renowned designer, who apprenticed at the age of fourteen for seven years in his grandfather's boatyard in England, endowed all his design work with a grace and elegance that has been rarely matched to this day.

Information that Jim has read states that the *Kawandag II* was on the lakes until 1938, but he and the friends he grew up with (Don Hodgins and Bill Schregardus) at the south end of the lake from the late fifties to the mid-seventies remember differently. They are sure that as kids they used to climb all over her as she sat in the Muskoka Sands Inn Boathouse with a number of other classics, collecting mold and the largest wharf spiders imaginable. These boats, six or seven in all (including a Streamliner), were piled on top of one another like so much cordwood and forgotten for years. They never realized at the time that the boats on which they carved their names, in which they were

having their first romantic adventures, those old boats that they were sure were just junk, were in fact destined to be the classics that are so sought after today.

By 1922, the Ditchburn plant had expanded to a point where it could produce a total of eighteen launches a year—nothing compared to the big shops of the south but for an out-of-the-way area such as Muskoka this was quite a feat. By 1926, Ditchburn

could not keep up with the ever-increasing orders from the States and opened another plant in Orillia, Ontario, twenty miles (32km) to the south. Employing 133 men between the two plants, the Ditchburn Company was now exporting more than half their vessels to America. Access to the Great Lakes was made easier by the Trent Waterway system that had been developed at their back door in Orillia, thus greatly simplifying the logistics of product delivery.

ABOVE: Special boats deserve special homes. Here, *Corsair*, a 1939 35-foot (10.7m) Herreshoff launch, sits placidly in her own boathouse.

49

NEAR RIGHT:
The traditional Chris-Craft colors of navy blue, crimson, and white are reflected in this runabout's color scheme—red mahogany, white caulking, and navy blue trim.

FAR RIGHT:
Golden Girl, a 1929 Fay & Bowen design, drifts quietly in the setting sun.

Building went along well until the thirties, when, due to the far-reaching effects of the Depression, orders for runabouts and launches started to fall off. The company advertised eleven models—eight runabouts and three cruisers—in 1931, but the number of boats actually sold was not high. As the Depression years moved forward, Ditchburn, with their two plants and extremely high overhead, could not keep up. They were forced to sell the Orillia plant and move back into the original Gravenhurst facility. This put them in direct competition with Greavette and the twelve other major builders in Muskoka. In the face of these and other pressures, Ditchburn was forced to reorganize.

Like most boat builders hard hit by the economic crash, Ditchburn now began a five-year struggle to stay alive in the boat business. After closing their doors for a short time, they reopened in 1933 as the Ditchburn Boat and Yachting Co., Ltd., in the old plant in Gravenhurst. They now concentrated on smaller utility boats and launches, but also bid on larger cruiser orders. One of their last large orders came in 1935, when they were contracted to build the *Birch Bark*, a 52-foot (15.8m) cruiser.

In 1936 the company was reorganized once again but could not keep its head above water. Finally, in 1937, the bank called in a $10,000 loan and the company closed. Jim's grandfather, William G. Ogilvie, was selling Ditchburn boats in the end and was quoted as saying, "The bank's action was both premature and unjustified as operations were picking up satisfactorily." In the end, Herb Ditchburn went on to help with the design of steel boats for the war effort with Gar Wood in Trenton and invented a welding technique that won him a prize in the Lincoln Memorial Foundation Competition in 1947. Ditchburn died in 1950, leaving a legacy of beautifully handcrafted mahogany masterpieces that can still be seen plying the waterways of Canada and the States. Given the quality of their construction, it seems likely that they will continue to be seen for many years to come, a credit to their designer and builder.

SPORT
UTILITIES

THE WOODY LETS LOOSE

Before the "runabout" made its official appearance as the motorboat of choice for having fun on the water, there existed a period during which utilities were modified for pleasure use. Bigger engines were added, design lines were tightened, and equipment such as the Chris-Craft Aquaboard allowed vacationers to enjoy the beginnings of waterskiing. As the demand for sporting boats increased, a whole new crop of boatyards was established and the race was on to use the improving technology to capture the blossoming recreational market.

Sport utility is a blanket term that covers this group of craft. A sport utility is not a barrelback, definitely not a cruiser, and usually features an open cockpit. Simply put, it is a utility vessel that is used for sport, whether fishing, hunting, waterskiing, or just poking around. The length was generally 14 to 23 feet (4.3–7m), with emphasis on stability and practicality. All sorts of power plants were used to make them go, depending on who owned the boat and exactly what it was used for. Often used by the kids while mom and dad used the "big boat" (the mahogany barrelback), sport utilities were great training boats for the younger generation to get its feet wet.

The smaller sport boats were now starting to make their way onto the market. With the advent of the gas outboard motor, the rowboat could now become a motorboat. The benefit of using an outboard for fishing and the like was clear—the extra space saved by not having an engine cover in the middle of the boat and the ability to get into shallow water (such as the Hoc Roc River at the southern end of Lake Muskoka) were great advantages. In fact, given the state of the world economy during the early thirties, these kinds of vessels were even more

OPPOSITE: *Elgin*, a 1931 21½ foot (6.6m) Dodge cruiser, cuts through the water at full speed.

53

popular because of their ability to help provide food for the family. Any purchase that could put meals on the table was worth the expense. Chris-Craft, Fetthall, Barnes, Carling, Peterborough, Grew, and a host of others recognized this, and all were soon producing open runabouts that could be used for fishing and hunting.

In 1931 the Johnston Motor Company of Peterborough, Ontario, was producing a nice sport package for $235—a 15-foot (4.6m) lapstrake with its own 3-horsepower outboard engine. They were also producing a 17-foot (5.2m) model with the buyer's choice of eight different motors, from 2 horsepower up to 32 horsepower. Prices for these motors ranged from $155 for their 2-horse to $420 for their Sea Horse v45. Also in Peterborough was the Peterborough Canoe Company, most commonly known for their production of quality canoes since the late 1800s and now building eleven different styles of canoe and motorized runabout.

LEFT: Classic runabouts, the Gar Woods were known for their clean lines and quality workmanship.

BELOW: A decorative brass panel surrounds the instrument cluster of this classic Hacker. The embossed leaf pattern is reminiscent of motifs made popular by the arts and crafts movement, which redefined the decorative arts and influenced all kinds of design around the turn of the century.

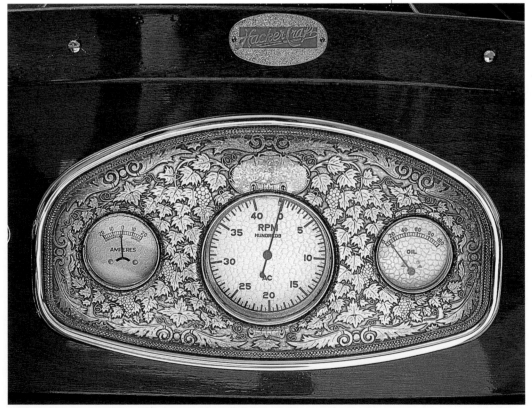

The Outboard Motor Corporation of Milwaukee was also in the hunt for the consumer's buck in 1931, selling a formidable line of outboards. One division of the company, Elto, produced "battery ignition outboard motors" from $2\,3/4$ horsepower up to their big "Senior Quad" and "Big Quad" at 35 and 40 horsepower, respectively. The other division, Evinrude, produced "Magneto ignition outboards" from four horses to forty. The company at the time was advertising no less than twenty-two outboards at prices in line with the other two manufactures, Johnston and Lockwood. Lockwood, incidentally, was producing four outboard engines at the time: 2-, 7-, 12-, and 45-horsepower motors.

By the mid-thirties, Chris-Craft was producing a number of utility model boats. The standard utility was advertised as "the lowest priced big utility boat on the market, powered by a 55 horsepower motor providing speeds of up to 26 mph [42kph]." The 21-foot (6.4m) Deluxe Utility (which came in three different models) was what we would refer to as a sport utility. It was advertised by Chris-Craft as "the swankiest

OPPOSITE: The making of beautiful wheels like this one was an art in itself. Steaming, shaping, and exhausting finishing were required to produce a wheel as pleasing to the eye as it was to the touch.

BELOW: A Gar Wood runabout at full throttle and full plane skims across the surface of the water.

boat of this type built, useful for every member of your family—for fishing, swimming, thrill rides, water sports or vacation needs, you can't make a better investment." Powered by your choice of a 55-, 75-, or 93-horsepower motor, these boats could reach speeds of 26, 29, or 32 miles per hour (42, 47, and 51.5kph). Also in production the same year at Chris-Craft was their Sea Skiff model. More than simply a utility, the Sea Skiff not only made recreation possible, but enabled one to do so in greater comfort, with more room and longer range. With a hull painted white and a huge expanse of room behind, these 23¹/2-foot (7.2m) models were the company's answer to quality, affordability, and comfort in a utility-style design. An advertisement at the time claimed:

Like every model in the great Chris-Craft fleet this boat was created for a definite purpose and to meet a specific need. For years, yachtsmen have sought a big, powerful, open type boat for deep-sea fishing, commuting, cruising and general utility use. The new Chris-Craft Sea Skiff is the answer to that demand.

Throughout the thirties and the forties Chris-Craft continued to provide their utility, sportsman, and Sea Skiff models with little change to any of them from year to year, while maintaining the quality and style that had become an integral part of the Chris-Craft name.

An interesting conflict arose about this time. Chris-Craft had always advertised that their vessels were made of Philippine mahogany. This claim was repeated so often that it became part of public knowledge, the marine equivalent of "Corinthian leather."

LEFT: The *Miss St Lawrence* powers through the water with grace and style.

ABOVE: Builder's plates, like these from Chris-Craft and Hacker Craft, provided pertinent information on each boat built. Rather than relying on memory or paperwork, sailors could refer quickly to the builder's plate when ordering parts or arranging for service. These days, the most important information they contain is the hull number.

59

Unfortunately, it seems that there really was no such thing as Philippine mahogany. What was really being used to build Chris-Crafts was a wood from the Philippines called indoako wood. After this inaccuracy had been exposed, advertising was released to the public explaining the misunderstanding and quoting the lumber importer's defense of the wood, saying, "It has lighter weight, greater freedom from splitting, less absorption of water and at a cheaper cost." In effect, it possessed the same character as the Central and South American mahoganies but proved to be the better wood. The public forgave this small slip in advertising and continued to purchase their Chris-Crafts.

Other builders of the era continued to provide faster-moving craft, such as Higgins of New Orleans, with their 26-foot (7.9m) sport cruiser; Truscott of Michigan, with nine different utilities and

LEFT: A fine example of a utility launch, this prowler, *Black Jack*, is perfect for ferrying guests and supplies to and from the summer cabin on the lake, or for just racing around for the fun of it.

BELOW: Once the open cockpit of the utility was closed over, the move toward a fast, sleek, fun-to-drive boat was on.

sport boats; and, on the West Coast, Western Boat of Tacoma, Washington, which provided fast tuna tenders to the fishing fleet of the Pacific

Northwest. The Muskoka builders of this period were still supplying working craft to the public and, in particular, their "Streamliner" launches

to the rich. It is typical of these craftsmen that they seemed unable (or unwilling) to adapt to the innovations in the industry that were being

taken advantage of in the States. These old-style builders were quite happy with the money they were being paid to produce their custom-made

launches and were not willing to attempt mass production like those south of the line. Call it the romance of the wood, an inability to sacrifice

individual attention to detail, or stubborn clinging to old ways of doing things. However it is regarded, a definite divergence is evident here—the boatyards of the north generally didn't conform to the changes in the industry, while those in the States that had previously produced similar craft for years now moved with the times and vaulted ahead. By incorporating the newest building techniques and designs, American builders such as Chris-Craft, Gar Wood, and Century found widespread success, fame, and influence, while most of the individual Canadian builders sank into obscurity.

LEFT: A trio of vintage boats sit alongside a Lake George, New York, wooden dock. In the foreground is *Dawn*, a reproduction Hacker built by Bill Morgan.

THE WAR EFFORT

⤳⤳⤳

WOODIES AT WAR

Just as World War I affected the boating industry by encouraging rapid improvements in marine technology, so too did World War II affect the industry, although more than just a technological influence was felt. The Second World War played a major part in pulling the boat builders out of the hole that had been dug for them during the Great Depression. As Canada and then the United States entered the conflict, boat builders large and small were called on to help in the effort.

In the early forties the Muskoka builders, like their American counterparts, began producing boats at the request of the military. Typical of the many small Canadian builders, the Ditchburn Boat Company had been struggling along at a snail's pace since 1931. After providing quality utility craft and other types of vessels for the common man for years, the company found that the Great Depression meant the common man was no longer buying boats from them, or from anybody else, for that matter. With two-thirds of its employees laid off and only two orders for boats in 1932, Ditchburn had little choice but to rename, restructure, and try to survive. Ditchburn finally closed up shop and in 1938 went to help Gar Wood in Trenton with the building of boats for the Navy. The move was a good one, because within a year, Gar Wood was going to need all the help it could get.

At the beginning of the war there was a rush to buy boats as people realized that if they didn't order right away, they might not be able to get what they wanted. They were right, of course, because by the time the war machine got humming in the summer of 1940 there were no

OPPOSITE: Built during the Second World War, this 35-foot (10.7m) Matthews with open aft deck and ample interior cabin space can handle heavy seas and still bring in the fish.

65

ABOVE: A wooden patrol boat cruises through New York Harbor just after World War II.

more pleasure craft being built in Muskoka. All the builders in the area were concentrating on war orders, and it seemed like everyone in the Muskokas was involved in the war effort. The Dukes of Port Carling were building 25-foot (7.6m) diesel motor cutters as well as rowing whalers as part of their war contracts. Minett-Shields was building utilities, and among the boats that Greavette was building for the Air Force were three 30-foot (9.1m) crash boats and three 40-foot (12.2m) bomber range patrol boats. Johnston was also involved in building six forward-drive boats for the Air Force, but because they had initially been designed for use in the clear waters of the Muskokas, the stems had to be changed from wood to aluminum so that the salt-water parasites would not destroy them. The Port Carling Boat Works, another Johnston company, was also producing boats for the war. They, too, had an order to build 25-foot (7.6m) motor cutters and later went into partnership with Minett-Shields to build a number of Fairmiles, a 46-foot (14m) harbor craft, and a number of 126-foot (38.4m) mine sweepers.

The Fairmile was a popular ship with the military, a fact that led to Greavette being contracted to build a total of nine Fairmiles for the Navy at a plant they leased in Toronto. Designed by the Fairmile Company of Great Britain, the Fairmile was a 112-foot (34.1m), B-class motor launch, a coastal craft that had room for twenty crew, weighing 75 tons empty and 145 tons loaded. With three heads and one shower, it was definitely not your usual Muskoka runabout. Powered by twin 671 GM diesels, the Fairmile could make a respectable twelve knots at 14 gallons an hour. Built of double diagonal mahogany and white oak frames, she was a very tough little ship. Approximately eleven of these ships were built in the Muskoka area, with a few still being built as the war ended. As mentioned, Minett-Shields in conjunction with the Port Carling Boat Works were also contracted to build the Fairmile at their shops in Port Carling, Orillia, and Honey Harbor.

William G. Ogilvie was not only an explorer of the wild rivers of the north but was also a very knowledgeable yacht broker before the war. He spent much of his time during the war inspecting the vessels being made by Canadian boat-building companies. As a government inspector, it was his duty to inspect any independently contracted military craft: assault boats, Baily-Bridge pontoons, and 55-foot (16.8m) cargo lighters, as well as the Fairmiles and other vessels. At the end of the war, having been in the position to know where these vessels could be found around the world, he advised buyers who had paid next to nothing for these four-year-old boats (usually around $25,000) on how to convert them to pleasure craft—if they dared. The following is an excerpt from an article he wrote in *Boating* magazine in 1945, discouraging the conversion of the Fairmile:

"But surely it wouldn't cost anything like those figures to convert a Fairmile to a peace time yacht," you exclaim. Well, there are a lot of things to be done. In the first place you would want to replace the twin 500 horsepower gas Hall Scott engines unless you were the president of some oil company. So you cast about for a couple of 100 to 200 horsepower diesels to take their place. After you have had the decks cleared of the gun emplacements, depth charge mountings, etc., and begin to study the below decks layout you find that you only have room for a crew of ten and accommodation for only three or four guests including the owner. So cabins must be altered, practically from stem to stern. Then you find that everything is below decks, like a house with the living quarters in the basement but with no ground floor. So plans for a deck house are studied, one large enough to provide a lounge and a dining salon. When that is completed, the new mahogany deck house doesn't match the grey and white camouflaged hull and topsides so the decks are sanded down and refinished natural and the topsides are painted white. By this time it is beginning to look like a yacht but it still has a rather funny stern. If it is ready for the boating season, which I doubt, then you must look out for a crew, because a 112-foot [34.1m] boat isn't a one man proposition.

Further on in the article he does give good recommendations for converting other craft, such as the RCAF crash boats (used to pick up crashed pilots) and the tenders being built by Johnston. He notes, "Many of these have sedan tops and need only a coat of paint to turn them into useful runabouts," and continues, "along the eastern seaboard these little diesel powered tenders will make someone happy. Built under the closest supervision, with grown to shape stems and knees and generously nailed and bolted with the best copper rivets and naval bronze bolts, these boats should be good for years to come."

The United States was in much the same position during the war: building boats for military use, but on a much larger scale. Chris-Craft was still producing runabouts and cruisers for the public but the order had to be in early to get one for the season ordered for. Advertising on the cover of their 1942 "Chris-Craft in US Defense" sales catalog states:

These photographs of Chris-Craft built boats for defense have been released for publication by government authorities. We take pride in serving this great cause. . . . We are building and have built boats for the United States Army, United States Navy, and for other departments as rapidly as ordered. . . . Defense needs come first with Chris-Craft. The new models shown on the following pages were designed and built without interrupting our defense activities. Production is limited by defense demands on our facilities.

Chris-Craft, as always, was keeping up to date with their advertising and making sure that the public knew they were doing their share. The following ad illustrates the company's advertising savvy particularly well:

We could go on and tell you many more fine things about Chris-Craft. But we should like to close with the record of just one Chris-Craft—the Bonny Heather—a peacetime 32 footer [9.8m] Chris-Craft Cruiser that was "conscripted" for the evacuation of Dunkirk by the British.

ABOVE: PT95 was a prototype patrol boat built for the U. S. Navy by Huckins during World War II. Demands for defense vessels during the 1940s meant that boat manufacturers produced fewer personal craft.

Better still, we'll let you read the words of Lieutenant Charles Waterman Read, an officer in the Royal Navy, convoy leader and commander of the Bonny Heather. "I want to tell you about the Bonnie Heather, a Chris-Craft Cruiser which participated in the evacuation of Dunkirk. I can't even begin to describe the hell under which the operations were carried out—bombed, machine gunned, shelled, caught in parachute flares and bombed—the little ship was certainly built in a lucky zone, and dodging and twisting never once let us down, loaded as she was. The Bonny Heather stood up to it like a Trojan, made seven complete round trips, Ramsgate to Dunkirk, after filling up transports (laying off) from the beaches. About 60 men were carried on each trip, except the last, and on that one the number was close to eighty. I selected the Bonny Heather as a leader of a convoy of motor boats. Believe me, the choice was justified."

Chris-Craft had begun bidding on contracts in the forties and began testing with the Navy department the same year. The government began giving Chris-Craft orders for engines in 1941. The orders were small at first compared to the size of what companies such as Wheeler and Higgins were getting, but they were the perfect size to sort out the government paperwork that came with this new territory. Chris-Craft supplied engines to the larger builders in the beginning, including the Palmer-Scott Company of New Bedford and the Southwest Harbor Boat Company of Maine. It was only a matter of time, however, before the orders for full vessels would start coming in. Soon after the raid on Pearl Harbor, Chris-Craft got its first large order, for 1025 36-foot (11m) landing boats. The work was to be divided between their three large plants— 260 for Algonac, 295 for Holland, and 170 for the Cadillac plant. Chris-Craft actually offered the Navy department full use of their engineering staff and production regimens. The fact that Chris-Craft was already outfitted for the mass production of pleasure boats made them well suited for taking on military orders. Of course, sales for all the manufacturers that were working to support the war effort were way up, in some cases as much as three times the norm for the period.

Plywood was to be used in the building of these hulls, but this posed no real problem for Chris-Craft. The fabrication of these vessels was probably among the first major marine applications of plywood. Each craft was powered by a Gray Marine diesel engine producing 225 horsepower. Chris-Craft was rewarded for their efforts in 1942 with one of the Navy's highest honors when their plants in Algonac, Holland, and Cadillac were decorated with the Navy E Pennant. Usually given only to members of the services, this award was now, by special permission of the president, being given to companies that had fulfilled the necessary qualifications. The Navy E was the highest reward a company or regiment could receive for production excellence, superior service, loyalty, and devotion to duty. The company was also thanked in a number of letters, such as the one from Rear Admiral E. L. Cochrane:

To the men and women of Chris-Craft's Algonac, Holland, and Cadillac plants. . . . On the completion of your 10,000 landing craft for the Navy, it is appropriate for the bureau of ships to congratulate you for your outstanding accomplishment, and to express its appreciation for your splendid contribution to the war effort.

Gray Marine, the engine supplier to Chris-Craft and other builders, was also honored with the Navy E Pennant, for the first time in 1942 and again in 1944.

Soon after the first order was received, Chris-Craft took another large boat order from the Navy. The Navy requested that they build 105 Navy harbor boats, 725 personnel ramp boats, 400 vehicle ramp boats, and 200 additional personnel ramp boats. Since Chris-Craft had years of experience mass-producing pleasure craft, the Navy made all these requests rush orders. It is a testament to the company that they were all filled, and filled on time.

RUNABOUTS

⤟⬥⤞

STYLE OVER SUBSTANCE

If you mention the term *runabout*, the image that comes to most people's minds is that of a dark mahogany barrelback or "cigar boat" cutting a path through the water, throwing spray to the sides from the bow and passing at great speeds. As noted earlier, the term was initially given to any type of boat under about 30 feet (9m) that had either an inboard or outboard engine. With the multitude of designs and styles that have evolved over the years, the term has narrowed somewhat to distinguish a particular class of boats. It has now come to mean any boat, usually made of mahogany, with an enclosed engine and an open cockpit. Because this is the general understanding of the term, "runabouts" as they are presented here will refer specifically to that style of vessel.

The runabout represents the perfection of certain building techniques and the application of technological breakthroughs that today are commonplace. As the automobile changed from an uncomfortable mode of transportation that riders simply endured to a sleek and luxurious vehicle that could be a pleasure to drive, so too did the boat evolve and change over time. The Great Depression came to a close, the Second World War began to reignite global economies, and the populace began to clamor for vessels that were fun, flashy, and fast. People needed diversions and for the first time in many years they had the money to pay for them. The main focus of the boat builders now was to produce vessels that were sleek, speedy, and beautiful. Boats were no longer just workhorses or ferries; boat owners were demanding craft that were status symbols to be pampered and shown off to friends, business associates, and neighbors. The boat builders of the time were now producing

OPPOSITE: As it races ahead of the weather, there is little doubt that this vessel can keep up the pace. The dramatic striping of the of the teak planks with white caulking caulking emphasizes the detailed craftsmanship involved in building classic runabouts.

71

BELOW: Gar Wood
was well known for
his exacting attention
to every detail. This
high standard of quality
can be seen in every
aspect of this triple-
cockpit runabout, from
the impeccable wood-
work to the luxurious
interior upholstery.

all styles of craft, particularly runabouts, but it should be kept in mind that this is also the time that the enclosed cabin cruiser was really starting to make its debut. Although there was always a niche in the market for the open runabout, the cabin cruiser as we know it today was beginning to take over the public's opinion of what a family boat should be.

To remain in the market, the major builders were now producing both types of boats. Not surprisingly, the smaller builders of Muskoka more or less stuck with what they knew best—the open runabout. This trend from smaller to larger boats is clear when one looks at the ratios of runabouts to enclosed cruisers produced by one of the most prolific companies, Chris-Craft. In 1929 Chris-Craft was putting out eighteen models of craft; six of the models were cabin-style cruisers and eleven models were runabouts. In 1926 eleven models were offered and all were

runabouts, with one 26-foot (7.9m) sedan. In 1931 Chris-Craft offered thirty-seven models, with twenty-three of them enclosed cruisers, and in 1939 they offered a staggering ninety-nine different models, with thirty-four utilities and runabouts being built! If you define "runabout" as we have done, that year actually saw only fourteen runabout models.

The Depression apparently had little effect on the hobby-turned-enormous-boatworks created by millionaire speedster Gar Wood. Wood's boats were now in as much demand as those of the rest of the major builders, and his factory at Algonac could not keep up with the demand for his racy craft. Consequently, Wood decided to build a larger factory that could satisfy the market's requirements. When it was completed in 1930, this factory at Marysville, Michigan, could build twelve hundred quality custom boats a year. Two basic models were the mainstays of the line, a 28-foot (8.5m) runabout and a 22-foot (m) runabout, with additions to either available on request. The 33-foot (10.1m) runabout (the "stock version" of the famous Baby Gar racer) was also still being built at Algonac. In 1930 an 18-foot (5.5m) runabout and a 25-foot (7.6m) triple cockpit were added to the line. All of these had the distinguishable Gar Wood-designed folding "V" window and swept-back lines that were inspired by Wood's passion, racing.

In the February 1931 edition of *Canadian Power Boating*, Gar Wood advertised that they were producing eight runabouts, three sedans, four limousines, two Landaus, and one cruiser. With sixteen other boat builders advertising on the same two pages, Gar Wood stands out among all of them for the amount of power used to move their craft. While most vessels of the time were using 30- to 140-horsepower engines, Gar Wood was packing 75 to 500 horsepower into their boats' engines. Of the eighteen models the company was offering, twelve could do more than 40 mph (64kph), with seven of those doing more than 50 mph (80kph). Of the 116 individual boats advertised in *Boating's Standardized Boat Buyers Guide* for 1931, only a Chris-Craft sedan and two Sachau runabouts could do 40 mph (64kph). The rest were slower, reemphasizing the fact that Wood loved power and built the fastest boats available to the public.

Wood always had his foot in the racing door but business was business and in 1935 business dictated that he should build a line of utilities along with his custom runabouts. The year 1938 saw the introduction of the elliptical Streamliner, a gorgeous triple-cockpit runabout. By using a V-drive gear, Wood was able to mount the engine in the rear of this 22-footer (6.7m), resulting in a faster boat that needed less horsepower. Recognizable by their barrelback shape and sometimes canoe-shaped sterns, everything about these sleek craft said speed, not to mention their power—these babies could reach speeds of up to 50 mph (80kph), with some of the Streamliners powered by V-12s that produced up to 350 horsepower. The name was well chosen; there were no straight lines aboard these vessels and their shape is indeed severely streamlined. Their bows were usually of a bullnose type, with the rounded hull raked aft. They seemed strange looking when first introduced but were quickly accepted by the boat-buying public.

The 1947 Chris-Craft 20-foot (6.1m) Custom Runabout, although not as drastically streamlined and not advertised as a Streamliner, is a clear attempt to keep up with the success of these models by rounding out the traditional runabout hull. It is actually rather difficult to discern who first came up with the Streamliner design. In Muskoka at around the same time, Greavette built a Streamliner designed by John Hacker and also a Sheerliner designed by Douglas Van Patten. With these two now-famous designers having had their say in the specifications, the Streamliner and the Sheerliner were and are still among the standouts of the wooden classics.

The Horace Dodge Boat and Plane Company of Newport News, Virginia, and their sales office on 52nd Street in New York continued to concentrate on open runabouts. As in the past, the builders of the time were putting fold-down tops on their vessels but the cockpits were still open and the boats they were producing were still classified as runabouts. Although they were building cruisers by 1931, their main business was the Dodge watercar. Yes—this vessel was manufactured by an automobile company, and it showed in such noticeable additions to the runabout as an automobile steering wheel and hood ornament. This hood ornament—a bare-breasted "Flying Lady" cast from nickel with her wings spread backward to caress the leading edge of the foredeck, her silver legs extending down the stem—was proud enough to grace any sailing ship.

Horace Dodge Boat and Plane Company used five different basic hull designs with numerous cabin and deck configurations to produce a variety of boat models in 1931, ranging from the well-known Watercar to the "Sea Lyon 30" to a 45-foot (13.7m) double cabin cruiser. These classics were powered by Lycoming engines with a power spread from 40-horsepower engines in the smaller models up to a combined 600 horsepower (twin 300s) in their 45-foot (13.7m) double cabin cruiser. Advertised in a 1930 edition of *Boating Business* as "a miracle of per-formance," their 21-foot (6.4m) runabout "rides like an airplane in the water that makes bigger boats run for cover." These models—recognized on the water by their sharply raked aft windows, their flagstaff centered on their navigation light (mounted just forward of the front window), and their white waterline stripe flaring wider as it ran forward—were priced in a range that made them affordable to the average boat enthusiast.

The Horace Dodge 16-footer (4.9m), with its open aft cockpit and a top speed of 25 mph (40kph), was equipped with "self-starter and electric lights" and was priced at $945 F.O.B. factory. The 21-foot (6.4m) runabout, with its window-enclosed aft cockpit behind the engine, was equipped with a Lycoming straight eight that produced 125 horsepower and was priced at $2100. The 25-footer (7.6m) had a little less power but was able to carry six people. Their top-of-the-line production model at the time was their 28-foot (8.5m) runabout at $3700. Powered by a 12-cylinder, 300-horsepower engine, this Dodge model could easily break 45 mph (72kph), and was advertised with the claim "Unusually luxurious in equipment, modern in streamline beauty, the Dodge 28 ft [8.5m] models present the utmost in boating value."

That same year, the Hacker Boat Company of Mt. Clemens and Detroit, Michigan, was advertising runabouts in the 24- to 30-foot (7.3–9.1m) range, and had been advertising their runabouts since 1914, when the company began. After a few years of successful experimen-tation with the likes of race enthusiasts such as Chris Smith and Gar Wood, John L. Hacker had opened the Hacker Boat Company. As stated earlier, this remarkable man was designing hulls and complete vessels for almost everyone in the business. His clients and coworkers ranged from Chris-Craft and Gar Wood in the States to Greavette and Minett-Shields in the Muskokas, and Woodard-McRea Boatworks in Quebec.

LEFT: Inspiration from the auto industry is once again evident in the streamlined transom of this vintage runabout.

OPPOSITE: Docked quietly in its slip, *Royal Flush* is ready for a quick jaunt around the lake on a moment's notice.

LEFT: Runabouts with room for the family offered three cozy cockpits that sat six to eight people.

Recognizable by their distinctive streamlined profiles, Hacker vessels sported a look that made them appear speedy even when they were sitting still—a look that other companies building wooden boats wanted to emulate. Greavette of Muskoka had Hacker sign on exclusively in Canada as their designer from 1933 to 1937, resulting in a series of very streamlined, fast hulls. One of the real beauties of Greavette-built Hacker design was the 18-foot (5.5m) Greavette "Flash." This model had a main two-seater cockpit set far aft of the engine, with a rumble seat forward in the bow that could be opened and closed at will. At 18 feet (5.5m) in length and packed with an 8-cylinder, this little racer was built for speed. The other models of that year had Hacker design written all over them—streamlining was the word with most of the builders in the mid- to late thirties, and John L. Hacker was the leading designer. Along with earning the likely credit for the design of the first Streamliner, this remarkable designer was the main leader in the design of the planing hull as we know it today. Hacker was a very busy man, so busy, in fact, that he required a leave of absence from the company at one point due to a nervous breakdown.

Chris-Craft's runabout models were similar to the rest of the pack after the war, as development and production of boats for pleasure was starting to build. With the upgrades and expansions that the war effort had demanded, Chris-Craft now had the room and facilities to build as

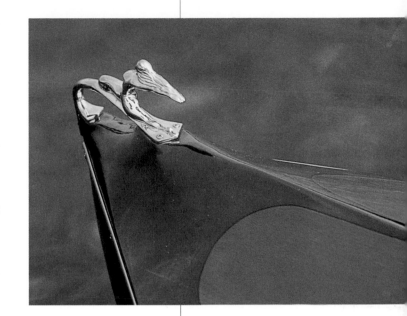

many boats in all sizes for which they had orders; the major problems were getting enough manpower and materials to do so. In June 1944 the Chris-Craft company sent out their first sales bulletin since the beginning of the war, stating that dealers should place their orders and enclose a $100 deposit for each craft ordered and that when "manufacturing resumes we will send you the models selected or the post war counterpart." Their orders until June 26, 1944, were worth more than $1.25 million but the war was not quite over. The company was still producing landing craft for the Navy department as needed, so civilian production was on hold. Little did they know at the time that the war was to go on for another year. The bulletin goes on to state:

It's a long time since you've heard from the factory but there's a good reason . . . we've still got our nose to the grindstone turning out 36' LCVP'S, LCPR'S and LCPL'S for the Navy at a rate that is beyond anything one familiar with the past production would expect. . . . [Dealer orders] were well along sometime ago but because of increased Navy schedules it was necessary to put a stop-work order on them on May 3rd; however it looks now as though we could continue after the fourth of July. . . . When are you going to resume the manufacture of standard Chris-Craft models? Upon the quick availability of raw materials and parts . . . but this much is certain—when the "Go" signal is received shipments can start within approximately sixty days. Will there be an increase in price? Boats are going to cost more due to the rise of labor and material. At this time it is unknown as to how much the advance will be. Cost studies disclose it could be anywhere from fifteen to thirty percent; however, it is our intention to hold prices as low as possible, consistent with good business.

On August 15, 1945, the war was over and the Chris-Craft plants at Algonac, Cadillac, and Holland, as well as the soon-to-be-opened plants at Jamestown, New York, and Chattanooga, Tennessee, were ready to go into full production to fill the ever-growing numbers of orders. Then the hammer fell once again. One of the major problems now was manpower at the factories. In August 1945, the same time the war ended, the American Federation of Labor (AFL) went on strike. Two months into the strike, an October 19, 1945, bulletin to dealers declared, "[The] latest news from the conciliation meetings looks hopeful for an immediate settlement. You will be advised promptly when the strikes are over."

LEFT: The *Miss Behave* is a stunning Gar Wood runabout kept in absolutely mint condtition.

ABOVE: *Little Miss Maple Leaf* is a replica of Harold Wilson's 1934 *Little Miss Canada*. The stylized bow cleat bears a striking Art Nouveau influence, much like the hood ornaments seen on many automobiles of the same era.

79

RIGHT: Multiple cockpits allowed designers and builders to show off their skills by balancing fine upholstery with dramatic decking details.

By early 1946 the strikes had ended and Chris-Craft was back in business, delivering backed-up orders and, almost immediately, making excuses for late deliveries. A Chris-Craft sales bulletin dated January 21, 1946, stated:

There are too many things over which we have no control that are interfering with scheduled delivery. For example, lumber of all kinds is being used up more rapidly than it is being received from the mills and other sources of supply. Yesterday, we ran out of exhaust manifolds, and the patterns that are necessary to have new ones cast are tied up in a one hundred and fifty-three day pattern makers' strike just ending. One of the big marine motor manufacturers had esti-mated a large shipment of various horse power motors. They still have not been received in quantity because there are no gear cases available for one size and no carburetors available in another. . . . In a few days the large supply of plate glass we have on hand will be exhausted due to no re-supply by the manufacturer due to strikes. This same condition applies to other supplies and materials used.

The bulletin of February 20, 1946, issued a plea to all dealers: "The most important thing to accomplish quickly is to get volume production of a variety of models flowing smoothly through the factories. This program is being seriously hindered by your requests for accessories, minor and major alterations, and special equipment." It continued, "Enclosed is a list of approved accessories for factory installation. For an indefinite period into the future these items are all that will be furnished."

Of approximately five hundred different parts and equipment offered in Chris-Craft's equipment catalog, this order from the factory cut back installation options to the basics only: anchor, compass, spotlight, name, and, on the larger 23-foot (7m) and 25-foot (7.6m) Express Cruisers, they would install the windshield wipers and head.

BELOW: *Baby Cakes,* a classic 19-foot (5.8m) barrelback Chris-Craft, is the very embodiment of the pre-war runabout.

By March of that year Chris-Craft had twenty production lines building boats, with another five to be put into operation. Even at this rate production was hurting. Again, getting skilled labor and providing the wood for the boats were the main problems and it's clear that the company was getting desperate. The March 26, 1946, sales bulletin to dealers stated, "The boss just came into my office and told me, 'that if we don't get more lumber within the next thirty days it will be necessary to shut down the factories.' This in spite of strenuous efforts,

including the travelling of a buyer throughout the United States. If amongst your acquaintances there are some in the lumber industry that have boat building woods available for immediate shipment, please let us know."

While it was usually the case that a yard would order lumber and materials based on design needs, this began to change in the face of the materials crisis. Now Chris-Craft's hull designs and finishes were altered to cope with the shortages in quality lumber. For the first time Chris-

Craft was beginning to paint not only their cruisers' hulls but also the hulls of their smaller runabouts. This was a radical departure from the traditional runabout look. Through the end of the thirties Chris-Craft's main sales catalogs for each year had proudly advertised, "Genuine Clear Philippine Mahogany is used in the bottoms, side planking, cabin sides and decks of Chris-Craft Cruisers. This wood is carefully selected, seasoned and matched by Chris-Craft, the world's largest buyers of this fine grade of hardwood. White Oak full-length keels, chines, and stem, forefoot and inter-mediate bent frames and transom frames are used in all models. Select Yellow Pine keelsons are used exclusively."

BELOW: Deep red mahogany bows reflect the similarity of design and construction materials that typifies classic runabouts.

Advertising that emphasized the quality of their materials became scarcer in the early forties, and it was mentioned less often in their annual sales catalogs. The first noticeable indicator of what was to come was the changing of "Select Yellow Pine" to simply "Fir." By 1946 any mention of the type of wood used was not to be seen again.

In sales literature today and in various used-boat price lists (such as the BUC Used Price Guide), the change in hull material is noticeable and dramatic. Under listings of hull material, where it had for the previous seventeen years said "MHG" (mahogany), it now said "WD" (wood) for all models. After all, the easiest way to cover up the wood shortage was to start painting more hulls. By 1948 only four models coming out of the Chris-Craft factories had a natural finish—the 17-foot (5.2m) Deluxe Runabout, the 20-foot (6.1m) Custom Runabout, the 18-foot (5.5m) Deluxe Utility, and the 25-foot (7.6m) Sportsman. The rest of the hulls were white, with different color combinations of bottom paint, boot stripe, and topsides that produced, in most cases, very aesthetically pleasing watercraft. Importantly, these early excursions into various color packages broke new design ground and laid the early foundation for the color schemes of later fiberglass boats.

83

BELOW: Hardwood decking, an enclosed engine, and an open cockpit are the hallmarks of the runabout—a sporty boat designed to be sleek, beautiful, and speedy.

The Century Boat Company of Manistee, Michigan, was producing runabouts of the 16- to 28-foot (4.9–8.5m) variety, designed once again by the ubiquitous Mr. John L. Hacker. Advertising in the 1930 issue of *Boating Business* was calling for dealers and distributors to come on board. The ad itself did not mention boats they were producing but spent more effort selling franchise information and boat plans. The ad read, "Prepare now to get your share of the profits that will accrue to the Century organization from now on! Racing Outboards—Pleasure Outboards and a brand new Inboard. Nineteen feet [5.8m] of fine craftsmanship from the board of John L. Hacker that will light the fires of desire in every boatman's heart."

The thirties were not big production years for the Century Boat Company; the real production began in the late forties with the Century Sea-Maid and the Resorter as their main models. These boats continued to be the company's central products until the mid-fifties, when they dropped the Sea-Maid and introduced their most popular model ever, the famous Century Coronado. While Century did build a 200-horsepower (powered by Gray Marine), mahogany 28-foot (8.5m) runabout in 1929, most of the craft they built until 1956 were powered with 75- to 140-horsepower engines. The boats from the early fifties until 1966 were made of lower-grade wood construction; like the other builders in the States, Century was having problems finding quality lumber but did not advertise this fact. In 1967, in a final "farewell to wood," Century built all their models of mahogany—the Resorter, the Arabian, and the Coronado. By 1969 there were no more mahogany or "wood" runabouts being built. Everything made by Century was constructed of fiberglass.

On another note, it is almost surprising that anyone could make any money selling prefabricated boats when such a variety of plans and designs were readily available. In 1935 Modern Mechanix Publishing Company published *How to Build Twenty Boats*, "Simple enough for amateurs yet exacting enough for professionals." This little paperback was full of designs and sketches for building boats, from small vessels to a 30-foot (9.1m) cruiser. One particularly cute 17-foot (5.2m) utility, with a total cost for lumber listed at about $100 to $125, "with a Ford model A engine converted to marine use will do speeds of up to 35 miles per hour [56.3kph]." The drive gear is a homemade V drive made from the sprockets of a motorcycle mounted on two separate shafts, with the shafts mounted through four Ford hubs. This rig is connected to the propeller at one end and to an "old car motor at the other." If you were a little more thrifty, you could mount your old washing machine motor (they seem to have been gas-powered) in the vessel and away you go. The message was definitely that if you wanted to boat badly enough, nothing could stand in your way.

As stated earlier, the Canadian situation was somewhat different. The smaller companies of the Muskokas continued to concentrate on smaller, individually built, mahogany runabouts. Whether this trend was due to the smaller number of orders, a stockpile of lumber, or just a tendency to stick with traditional methods is difficult to determine, although it is the authors' opinion that the latter reason was likely the most important. A 1931 article in *Canadian Power* mentions most of the major builders of runabouts being sold in the Canadian market at that time, including Barnes, Carling, Chris-Craft, Dis Pro, Ditchburn, Dowkes, Fetthall, Gar Wood, Gidley, Johnston, Midland, Peterboro, Richardson, Russell, Sachau, and Taylor. Of the 120 models these companies produced at the time, almost 70 were runabouts; the remainder were utilities and cruisers.

Greavette of Muskoka was one of the largest producers of fine wooden runabouts. The company originally started out in 1930 as Rainbow Craft, Ltd. Then Tom Greavette came to the controls, bringing with him thirty years of boat-building experience. That experience was nothing to sneeze at—he had grown up and built boats with the likes of Herb Ditchburn and Bert Minett. The company's first president, Gordon Lefebvre (a former Canadian executive at General Motors), was among the first in Canada to visualize and implement the production-line method of building boats. It's anybody's guess what effect this early high-speed production of boats in Canada would have had on the

OPPOSITE: The
demanding wood finish
and chrome brightwork
on early runabouts attest
to their status as luxury
boats. Unlike the more
practical utilities that
came before them,
these boats were meant
to be shown off.

present-day output of Greavette Boats if the Great Depression of the thirties had not dealt its staggering blow to Canada's (and everyone else's) economy. Ironically, it was this company's very inability to compete at a mass-production level that resulted in the distinctive Greavette style. The company's signature was a high standard of quality and individualized attention to detail that would have been impossible to maintain if they had mass-produced.

John L. Hacker headed the design team at Greavette from 1933 until 1937. The most outrageous design move away from the norm made in Hacker's time at Greavette was the design and production of the aforementioned Streamliner. For many years Tom Greavette had been dissatisfied with the performance of the fast runabouts. The V-bottoms rode well in the calm but pounded like crazy when the seas roughened. Round-bottom hulls, although good in a chop, in calm water rode on two waves that climbed the sides of the boat. Any crosswind would inevitably cause the spray to be thrown across the passengers—an undesirable state of affairs indeed. The Streamliner combined the best of these two major hull designs. Although the result was very beautiful, fine for touring the lake, and able to reach great speeds, at a practical level the rounded decks and sides were less than ideal. Boarding the Streamliner could be a bit tricky, especially for novices and passengers without their sea legs.

After Hacker's departure in 1937, another naval architect signed on. Douglas Van Patten, internationally renowned in the boat design field, was asked to design a hull that was a little more practical than the Streamliner of the previous few years. Although the Streamliner was still produced, this newest design—the Sheerliner—was better suited to the more casual recreational boater. The design of the Sheerliner was wider, less elliptical, and did not feature the canoe stern. Built in the 22-, 24-, 26-, 28-, and 30-foot (6.7, 7.3, 7.9, 8.5, and 9.1m) range, this new design was supplied with power ranging from 115 to 250 horsepower. The Sheerliner was constructed of white oak keel and frames, had seam battens of mahogany, and sported mahogany planking and transom. The top sides and deck were finished with eight to ten coats of high-quality spar varnish. The result was so easy on the eyes and performed so well that this runabout continued to be produced and eagerly bought until 1966.

During their time in the Muskokas, Greavette Boats owned or took over a number of different boat companies. In 1936 they took over the Disappearing Propeller Boat Company, and until 1958 they turned out more than three hundred of these small craft. They also went into partnership with Lyman of the United States and produced 13- and 15-foot (4.6m) lapstrake-type outboards and the "Islander" (as the inboards they also built were called), powered by a 25-horsepower Gray Sea Scout motor, which powered the boat along at about 15 mph (24kph).

The Gidley Boat Company of Penetang had a long history of boat building before becoming Grew Boat and Equipment, Ltd., in 1932. During the twenties the famous Gidley-Fords were produced in quantities and found approval with boat owners in Canada and many foreign countries. The engine used in these popular models was the famous Ford Model-T engine, which came shipped as a completely

ABOVE: The *Miss Lindy*, a Ditchburn triple cockpit built for speed, as evidenced by the very large engine compartment with double hatch access.

converted engine and transmission for marine use. The steering wheel was attached and the entire unit was ready for immediate installation into the waiting hull. Arthur Grew and Clarence Kemp took over control of operations in 1939, renaming the company Grew Boats, Ltd.

At the top of the list for expert craftsmanship in Muskoka was Minett and Minett-Shields, known for their extreme attention to detail and pursuit of perfection. Boats came out of their shops as close to perfect as one could get. H. C. Minett began building at a very young age. In his early teens on Lake Rosseau, Bert (as he was called) was building boats with great care. It is known that he completed at least two quality runabouts by the age of nineteen. By the age of twenty, he had completed a 45-foot (13.7m) steam launch while holding down a job at the same time.

For the majority of the twenties, Minett resided in Algonac, Michigan, where he learned from the master designer himself, John L. Hacker. After two years with Hacker and one year with renowned sailboat designer Steveson, Bert came home to open the H. C. Minett Motor Boat Works in Bracebridge, Muskoka. While there were runabouts on the lake by builders such as Duke and Barnes, the boats that came from Minett's yard were very special. Until the thirties it was common to see these boats going from lakeside lodge to lakeside hotel, commanded by a uniformed driver and his engineer, and carrying the smartly dressed passengers in the aft cockpit.

Minett's boat designer from 1911 to 1916 was Bert Hawker, fresh from his apprenticeship in England. His designs were recognizable by their long, sharp lines, vertical stems, and flush decks, a look very similar to what Ditchburn would later build with Hawker when he worked for him after 1919.s

An important date in Minett history is 1918, the first time Minett designed and produced vessels with a removable hatch forward of the engine. A review of the literature seems to confirm that this was in fact the first time that anyone had added a forward open cockpit for seating to these long sleek launches.

As with most of the builders in Muskoka, Minett fell on hard times in the late twenties and was only saved by the investment capital of a young man named Bryson Shields. In September of 1925, this investment was reflected in the formation of a new company, Minett-Shields. Known to be a stickler for perfection, Bert would not let a boat out of his shop till it was perfect, even if a boat had to go beyond the contract deadline into the penalty phase for completion. He would even go so far as to rip apart any offending aspects and start again if he thought that the work was not up to his exacting standards. An indication of the dedication and perfectionism of this man is found in his standard contract, which stated that the transom was to be of one piece of mahogany that would be steamed and bent to fit. To commit to a large and very expensive piece of wood like that was quite a feat, especially considering that other builders were having a hard time just finding enough mahogany to plank their hulls. Having built approximately 250 boats in the Muskokas, Minett-Shields was not the largest builder in history but will always be respected for the craftsmanship and beauty of its output.

BELOW: *Climax*, a 26-foot (7.9m) triple-cockpit Chris-Craft runabout.

RACERS

─◦◦◦─

THE NEED FOR SPEED

Once speed became a commonplace feature in the smaller recreational boats, it was only a matter of time before enthusiasts wanted to race them. While motorboats had always been raced in some form since their conception, the advances in engine technology made the pursuit of competitive speed more accessible. Regulations were established to restrict engine size for competition, drawing the line between gentlemen racers and their professional counterparts. Names such as Gar Wood, Chris Smith, Minett, Ditchburn, and Hacker began producing high-performance vessels for the professional circuit. Water speed records were broken on a regular basis as craft became light, streamlined shells designed to carry the largest and most powerful engines possible.

"Gentleman racing" began as tourists and visitors to the lakes and rivers of the continent discovered that it was rather exhilarating to jump into one of these souped-up babies and go fast. Very fast. These kinds of toys had once been the privilege of only the most exclusive buyers, but as mass production brought prices down, boating quickly became one of the continent's most popular recreations for the whole family. By the mid-fifties, estimates of boating's prevalence noted that there were approximately six million boats currently on American waters and that at least one out of every six people had enjoyed recreational boating. This increase in boating's popularity can be attributed to a number of influences, including the refinement of reliable and powerful engines, the increasing availability of quality fuels and fluids to use in those engines, and the development a variety of efficient hull styles and designs.

OPPOSITE: Racers like the classic cigarette boat epitomized the balance of power, grace, and, above all, speed of classic wooden speedboats. With their long, slim profiles and powerful engines, these vessels cut through the water like surface-skimming torpedoes.

91

Not surprisingly, the continual testing and pushing of limits in the fields of amateur and professional competition have contributed greatly to the refinement of boating performance over the years. Inboard and outboard racecourses have often been the proving ground where new innovations are perfected before becoming available to the general public. Fuels, lubricants, propellers, engine design, hull characteristics—all these variables and many more have been tweaked and experimented with over the years by people with a trophy and victory on their minds.

This is not to say that there is always a transfer of technology from the competitive arena to the slower and safer world of recreational boating. Obviously, the extreme demands of very high performance engines are far more rigorous than the needs of the average boater. Similarly, the strict requirements of aerodynamics result in hull designs that are completely impractical for casual, pleasure use. Rather, technology is tested, refined, and then tested again until the principles behind the technology are fully understood. At that point, the technology is transformed and applied to recreational vessels in a manner that is appropriate for their use.

The original internal combustion engines that powered the first motorboats were very different from the engines currently used. Engines had few cylinders, turned slowly, took up a disproportionate amount of

BELOW: Runabouts were becoming very stylized by the mid-1940s, a trend that is readily apparent in the torpedo-like shape of this 1946 Stan Young.

space for the amount of horsepower produced, and (at least initially) used a variety of fuels such as naphtha that were volatile, dangerous, and often unreliable. The newness of the sport and the fickleness of the technology meant that the first racing enthusiasts were a "live dangerously" lot who had to rely on their own technical expertise as much as they did their nerves. It didn't take long for the technology to evolve, however, and this early development can easily be charted by following some of the history of racing's two most valued prizes: the Gold Cup (American origin) and the Harmsworth Trophy (English origin):

1903	The Harmsworth Trophy is won by England at a speed of almost 20 mph (32kph).
1904	The first Gold Cup is won by the *Standard* with a top speed of over 23 mph (37kph).
1913	The Harmsworth Trophy is won by England for the last time when *Maple Leaf* takes it at an average speed of about 57 mph (92kph).
1914	The Gold Cup is won by *Baby Speed* with a top speed of more than 50 mph (80kph).
1920	Gar Wood wins the Gold Cup by reaching speeds of 70 mph (112.6kph) in *Miss America I*. She sports two Liberty engines that together deliver a total of 900 horsepower. It is noteworthy that after maximum engine displacement was dropped to 625 cubic inches by a rule change in 1922, the average speeds of Gold Cup contenders decreased significantly.
1920	Gar Wood wins the Harmsworth Trophy for the United States at speeds of more than 60 mph (96.5 kph). This was just the first of a series of victories achieved by the *Miss America* series, remarkable vessels that managed to hold on to the trophy until 1934. *Miss America X*, powered by four Packard engines providing a total of 6000 horsepower, reached speeds of more than 86 mph (138.4kph).
1949	Stan Dollars and *Skip A Long* win the Harmsworth Trophy by changing to a three-point style hull. Of course, 1500 horsepower pushing the boat to speeds of more than 94 mph (151kph) doesn't hurt either.
1950	*Slo-Mo-Shun VI* wins the Harmsworth Trophy by breaking 100 mph (161kph).
1956	*Miss Thriftway* wins the Gold Cup and amazingly exceeds 100 mph (161kph) for the entire 90 miles (145km) of the race.

As noted, there exists an intimate relationship between the refinement of technology on the racecourse and the application of those refinements in the field of recreational boating. Fuels, lubricants, and particularly hull and engine design have all benefited from the competitive arena. Fuels are chemically engineered to provide the best ratio of volume to volatility for any given set of demands. Lubricants are designed to withstand higher temperatures and resist chemical breakdown. Engines are now safer, more reliable, and more efficient due to improvements in such areas as compression, rotation, and cooling.

Equally important are the shape and properties of the hull that carries that engine. As engines became more powerful, the demands they placed on the physical spaces that housed them changed. Hull design is complicated by the myriad ways in which the exterior shapes of both hull and topsides can be altered to affect movement of the boat through both air and water—as speed increased, factors such as turbulence, resistance, and vibration became even more critical. Further variables include the weight and flexibility of the materials from which the hull is built, the manner in which the hull is weighted, and last (but certainly not least), the safety of the pilot. All these variables interact to affect a boat's maneuverability, seaworthiness, efficiency, and stability.

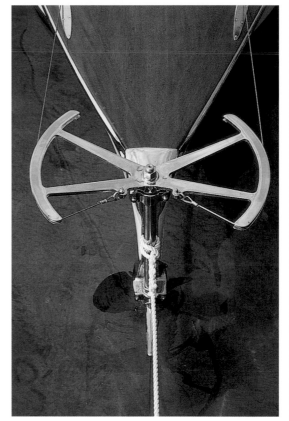

FAR LEFT: This dramatic racer was the 1924 Nevins Cup winner. Named *Baby Bootlegger*, it has all the spirit of the Roaring Twenties.

NEAR LEFT, TOP: Wire and cable steering set outside the transom allows for stylish steering at the canoe stern.

NEAR LEFT, BOTTOM: The outboard steering apparatus used on the fifties' more powerful racers were set aft of the transom for sharper and faster turns.

The first major hull innovation appeared during the early 1900s with the development of the "V" bottom, also referred to as a planing hull, which rapidly proved itself considerably more efficient—and certainly much faster—than the more pedestrian displacement hull. Displacement hulls were generally very deep, often rounded, and pushed the water out of the way by plowing through it. Such hulls were very stable but also very slow. Planing hulls took advantage of a shallow "V" shape that, given enough power, allowed a boat to ride predominantly above the surface of the water and thus reduce drag. Such hulls eat up a lot of fuel initially by requiring high output from their engines but are capable of reaching remarkable speeds. Much research, debate, and field testing has gone into the development of the planing hull over the years. Such research has determined that the advantages of the V-shaped hull are not felt until the hull reaches planing speed—typically around 10 mph (16kph). Beyond that speed fuel efficiency is vastly improved. This style of hull at first was limited to smaller racing boats but eventually began to be applied to larger vessels as engine technology improved and the amount of thrust needed to pick a large cruiser out of the water and into the planing position became more readily available.

The planing hull served the racing community very well until even greater speeds were needed to break the current records of the time. The 1922 rule change in the Gold Cup standards reduced the maximum engine displacement to 625 cubic inches (1587.5 cubic cm). The immediate effect of this capping of engine size was to reduce competition speeds, thus frustrating many racers of the day. Yet, since necessity is

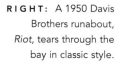

RIGHT: A 1950 Davis Brothers runabout, *Riot*, tears through the bay in classic style.

the mother of invention, it wasn't long before other hull configurations were being examined in the hopes that a change in the hull's shape would create more speed given the same thrust.

One avenue explored was the inverted V hull. The advantage of these hulls lay primarily in their shallow draft. Because less of the boat was in the water in the first place, the vessel could very quickly be brought up to the plane position. This made for spanking starts off the mark and gave the competitor valuable seconds at the start of the race. Fast pickup from a dead stop combined with a very shallow draft that allowed a careful pilot to enter shallow water (such as is found in river tributaries and beachsides) made this style of hull very popular with smugglers, bootleggers, rumrunners, and the police and government agents who had to catch them. The design never really caught on with the recreational boating public due to these vessels' unfortunate decrease in maneuverability and a general dissatisfaction with the aesthetics of the boat. Such hulls demanded very boxy topside designs that were too "unboatlike."

Another hull design that allows a boat to achieve great speeds is the hydrofoil. This design has existed for many years. It first appeared in 1919, when Alexander Graham Bell built a 60-foot (18.3m) hull supported by three foils (long, slender, ski-like fins) and driven by Liberty engines that powered two large air propellers. The vessel could reach speeds over 70 mph (21.3kph), a very respectable clip at that time. While this type of design certainly became popular in some parts of the country, it never really caught on with the general public.

LEFT: The *Delphine IV*, a replica of a 1925 26-foot (7.9m) Dodge fivestep hydroplane, was built in 1979. Hydroplane designs like this one were noted for their great speed, but they were also known for their inability to handle heavy seas.

THE FIFTIES

LIVING THE DREAM

The fifties were the Golden Age of recreational motorboating, a time when the family boat was as much a part of the American Dream as a white picket fence and a big highway land cruiser. The atmosphere of this decade is captured beautifully by the advertising found in boating magazines such as *Yachting* and *Motor Boating*. Chris-Craft was indisputably one of the industry's design leaders during this era, producing vessels that often had the same lines and fins as the owner's automobile parked by the pier. Boats became "cool" as they never had before. Pearl-inlay steering wheels, brightly colored plush leather (and plastic) interiors, dash-mount radios, and outrageous contours helped define the look of the time. Ironically, the design demands for unusual shapes and lines helped contribute to the eventual decline of the wooden motorboat industry by creating a need for lightweight, malleable materials such as fiberglass and epoxy.

Thanks to its large production facilities, Chris-Craft was rapidly becoming the design leader in the boating industry. Examining the many vessels that left these plants during the fifties provides a good sense of the types of designs that were gracing both American and Canadian waters. In 1950 the vessels coming out of the shops at Algonac, Holland, and Cadillac, Michigan, along with Caruthersville, Missouri, and Chattanooga, Tennessee, were a combination of the old-style barrelback runabout and the increasingly popular large cruisers and motor yachts. Runabouts were being produced in the 16- to 22-foot (4.9–6.7m) range with the traditional natural mahogany finish, but some design changes were beginning to hint at what was to come later as the decade progressed. The Riviera (16-, 18-, and 20-foot [4.9, 5.5, and 6.1m]), Deluxe Runabout

OPPOSITE: If you lived near the water in the 1950s, owning a boat was as normal as owning a car. And like the autos of the era, the boats are classics. Those lucky enough to own one have to work hard to keep them as pristine as this vintage Chris-Craft.

(17-foot [5.2m]), and Sportsman (18- and 20-foot [5.5 and 6.1m]) were all of a Streamliner style. Although not as aerodynamically sculpted as the Greavette models of Sheerliner and Streamliner, this design had enough of a following to move many boat builders to produce Streamline-influenced vessels.

Of the thirty-five boat models offered by Chris-Craft in 1950, only nine were of the runabout style. Boating as a family recreation was becoming more and more popular during this period, and the boating man was increasingly thinking about the comforts and amenities

that a family demanded. Consequently, cruisers, yachts, sedans, and various weekenders were becoming more in vogue. From the 21-foot (6.4m) Express Cruiser up to the 30-foot (9.1m) Sedan Cruiser, all of these models incorporated some creature comforts into their design, including heads and (in some of the larger boats) galleys. The Semi-Enclosed and Enclosed line of cruisers could all reach speeds higher than 30 mph (48.3kph), with the 28-foot (8.5m) Super Deluxe Semi-Enclosed Cruiser able to hit a peak speed of 40 mph (64.4kph) with its powerful twin engines.

With the exception of the 25-foot (7.6m) Sportsman, all the 1950 Chris-Craft vessels, from the 21-foot (6.4m) Express Cruiser up to the 62-foot (18.9m) Motor Yacht, came with painted hulls. The 19-foot (5.8m) Racing Runabout was finished red, white, and blue to reflect the postwar patriotism of the time. As previously discussed, however, this had as much to do with wood shortages as it did aesthetics or pride. Still, it was clear following the Second World War that the boat-buying public was willing to accept a painted hull, and Chris-Craft was never a company to turn its back on what the public wanted or expected. Although Chris-Craft had adopted the production-line method of building

LEFT: A 17-foot (5.2m) Chris-Craft utility runabout was a perfect family boat in 1957.

BELOW: A 1950 19-foot (5.8) Chris-Craft runabout (top) glides along at full plane.

boats, a compromise was struck between individual craftsmanship and mass production. Machinery was utilized to a great extent but for the final fitting the mallet, plane, and chisel were still used. The painting of a Chris-Craft was done with the same care. The only automation in the painting process involved spraying the primer coat; when dry, the hull would be painted by hand with three-inch brushes.

The sale of outboard motors was another area that Chris-Craft explored. In 1949 their outboard plant in Grand Rapids was in full production of the new 5.5-horsepower Challenger outboard. Added to production in 1950 was the 10-horsepower Commander. Unfortunately,

ABOVE: *Canadienne* (bottom), a 1952 25-foot (7.6m) Greavette runabout, speeds along with her bow high above the waves.

RIGHT AND OPPOSITE: The Capri proved to be one of Chris-Craft's most popular designs in the 1950s. With the force of 300 horsepower behind them, these vessels could really move along at a respectable 41 mph (66kph).

this was one instance where Chris-Craft did not follow its own example; the lack of variety and poor marketing resulted in very disappointing

sales. After millions of dollars in investment the plant was closed in 1953, making these rare outboard motors one of the great equipment

collectibles of recent marine history.

As the decade progressed, designs became more experimental and sometimes outrageous. As mentioned, there was a definite trend to

produce vessels that resembled the automobile fashions of the time. The 19-foot (5.8m) Silver Arrow, released in 1959, was a good example of

this type of style—sleek, silver, and speedy. Its most dramatic design feature was a set of wings set along the back "quarter panels," making it look

LEFT: The famous Chris-Craft Cobra is unmistakable from any angle. A classic mahogany raceboat with a then-cutting-edge fiberglass engine cover, the Cobra was a beautiful marriage of modern and old-fashioned design.

like a cross between a rocket and a race car. Powered by a single V8, the Silver Arrow could deliver speeds up to 42 mph (67.6kph). It was a popular boat for waterskiing because of its speed but also because of the ease with which it could be rigged for skiing—the stern featured a socket for a removable rangelight that could quickly be replaced with a ski tow pole.

Dramatically flared from stem to stern, the 1959 Chris-Craft Continental and Capri were two other beauties that reflected this optimistic age. With their flared wings aft and chrome-trimmed transoms, these models were about as close as Chris-Craft would come to putting a car

BELOW: Cashing in on the prosperity and optimism of the 1950s, boatbuilders began producing—and selling—more boats than ever before. Well loved and cared for, many vintage 50s cruisers are still around today.

on the water. The boat-as-car motif was given further emphasis by an exhaust configuration that resembled car exhaust systems of the time. These models could be purchased with either a landau hardtop with sliding aircraft canopy or with a soft convertible top. Both were fitted with an air scoop forward for ventilation to the cockpit. With the force of 300 horsepower behind them, these vessels could really move along at a respectable 41 mph (66kph).

The 1955 Chris-Craft Cobra was another striking model that stood out among its peers. Today it is much sought after and difficult to find. It ranks highly among serious collectors for two reasons. First, it is quite rare—production numbers were kept low, probably to reinforce its reputation as a specialty item. Second, it is a particularly beautiful boat that is at once sleek and graceful, but also very powerful. The Cobra features a distinctive, whale-like dorsal fin that protrudes from amidships to stern. This fin forms the hatch-cover for the single screw V8 engine. Finned boats such as the Cobra were not, of course, the exclusive domain of Chris-Craft. Revel Craft, Aristo Craft, Owens, and Dan Arena Co. were just a few of the builders creating craft with fins. Initially these efforts largely consisted of fiberglass details fastened to a predominantly wooden hull, but as time went on and resin technology improved, these types of boats began to be made entirely of fiber-reinforced glass.

RIGHT: The ubiquitous Chris-Craft logo is equally at home on a sculpted white topside as it is on a field of rich mahogany.

Chapter 9

LUXURY
CRUISERS

CONSPICUOUS CONSUMPTION

Throughout the history of the wooden motorboat, there have always been individuals for whom money is no concern and luxury is of paramount importance. Such people have often commissioned vessels and created a smaller market for custom-made yachts and cruisers that define opulence and the high life. Size does matter in these cases, and every effort was made to turn these beauties into homes away from home with all the amenities that go with them. Built mainly for ocean cruising and major inland waterways, these vessels established a continuing tradition of touring from yacht club to yacht club in order to see and be seen. The companies mentioned below are only a few of the yards and outfits to have produced luxury cruisers over the years. Of necessity, a brief overview such as this must be very selective; however, the authors would like to apologize for the companies that have been omitted. Huckins, Matthews, Burger, Richardson, Owens, Wheeler, and, of course, Chris-Craft were some of the major builders of fine yachts during the forties and afterward. Other notable companies include Grebe, Feadship, and Hatteras.

The Huckins Yacht Corporation consistently pursued the traditional boat-building techniques that have endeared their Fairform Flyer to the minds and hearts of luxury-conscious boaters. These twin-screw motor yachts were built in a series of standard models offering a wide range of variations and choice to the individual buyer. The basic feature of all Huckins models was the quadraphonic hull, a form of hull developed by Huckins in the twenties that fully planes at low speeds but is free from the chronic pounding and roll. Of the four basic hulls that Huckins offered in 1950, there were no fewer than a dozen cabin plans available, meeting almost anyone's ideal of what a yacht should be. They offered

OPPOSITE: The instrument panel for a twin-engine inboard craft. A quick scan of the dual meters provides the captain with the water temperature, rpm, and amps for each of the motors.

113

a very fast 33-footer (10m), four models in the 40-foot (12.2m) size, three models in the 45-foot (13.7m) size, and four models in the 48- to 52-foot (14.6–15.8m) size. The 48- and 52-foot (14.6 and 15.8m) models were generally diesel driven, with the engines mounted as close to the stern as possible. These vessels also used a Huckins Spiral Vee Drive, first introduced in 1934, to keep the noise of the engines down to a minimum.

S.J. Matthews founded the Matthews Company of Port Clinton, Ohio, a company known for its 40-foot (12.2m) Deluxe Sedan. Matthews had been developing this model since the thirties, and by 1950 the Deluxe Sedan model was available in two distinct interior plans. One of these incorporated an upper and lower berth in the main stateroom while the other featured built-in twin berths. This all-around boat was suitable for extended cruising as well as for fishing. Included in these popular models from the

THESE PAGES: The mighty *Aphrodite* was built in the late-1930s for commuting between the Wall Street office and Long Island home of one well-to-do New Yorker. Some fifty years later, the 72-foot (21.9m) yacht was found on dry dock in a state of terrible disrepair. It took three years to restore her to the pristine condition she now enjoys.

RIGHT: With covered cabin space forward and enclosed passenger room upstairs, *Tenango* taxis guests to and from waterfront hotels and businesses in the waters around New York City.

fifties was hot water on demand. Water was supplied by circulating engine cooling water through a separate water tank and then back through the engine, thus heating the water for immediate use. Also included was a shower-bath that with a flick of a switch provided hot water to the tub.

Richardson Boat Co. Inc. of Tonawanda, New York, had been building boats since the early 1900s. Throughout this period, their Little Giant model had been their mainstay. Another popular model was their 1920 28-foot (8.5m) Scout, powered by a four-cylinder motor with speeds up to 10 miles per hour (16kph). Richardson was one of few builders of that era to concentrate solely on cruisers, a fact that helped them establish their own niche over the years. By 1950 the Richardson fleet consisted of five models, a 26-footer (7.9m), a new 35-foot (10.7m) model, and three 31-foot (9.4m) boats that in 1949 proved to be their best-sellers. The 26-foot (7.9m) cruiser was virtually a copy of their earlier success with the Little Giant. Built of white oak framing with mahogany or cedar planking, the round bottom hull construction had rather sharp bilges and a large flat section aft that smoothed out the ride. Powered by a Gray 93 horsepower or a Chrysler 92 horsepower, they could get up to 30 mph (48.3kph) depending on the engine used and the conditions.

LEFT: *Speedwell* is a 33-foot (10.1m) cruisette built around 1925 by the Elco company of Bayonne, New Jersey.

Tastefully finished with all the amenities of the larger cruisers, these smaller cruisers made the opulence of cruising life more available to the average buyer. In the years to follow, Richardson became known for their larger yachts, boats that ranged from 36 to 46 feet (11–14m). Their 43-foot (13m) Double Cabin slept up to eight people in four separate areas on board. This beautiful vessel featured walk-around decks and mahogany handrails, and was fully equipped with electric refrigeration, cooking facilities, and twin 250-horsepower diesels. The Richardsons could be identified by the tasteful combination of natural-finished mahogany decks and painted cabin tops and hulls, creating a modern-looking small cruising vessel.

Burger of Manitowac, Wisconsin, has been building large cruisers and sailboats since 1907. From 1907 to 1937 they built primarily sailboats but then cut them out of the lineup almost completely in 1937. From that point on Burger concentrated mainly on large yachts that ranged from 45 to 72 feet (13.7–22m), as well as custom orders for even larger vessels. In 1921 they advertised their 36-foot (11m) Bridge Deck Cruiser, which combined the comforts and convenience of home with the ability to lounge outside under the convertible cover on the large bridge deck. With help from renowned designer John L. Hacker, these vessels were both

practical and beautiful. Burger built three models in 1950: 53-, 57-, and 67-foot (16, 17.4, and 20.5m) models. These grand yachts were powered by twin General Motors diesels able to produce 200 to 400 horsepower and reach speeds up to 15 mph (24kph).

Owens Yacht Co. of Baltimore, Maryland, had been advertising their yachts since the early thirties. Although they have always built boats of all size ranges—from 16 feet to 44 feet (4.9–13.4m)—in later years the company concentrated mainly on the production of 30- to 40-foot (9.1–12.2m) cruisers. Offering three 25-footers (7.6m), two 33-footers (10m), and featuring a 42-foot (12.8m) Flying Bridge in 1950, Owens was one of the largest producers of fine yachts. Incorporating copper-strengthened frames throughout their boats was one of the exclusive extras that

OPPOSITE: The handsome *Gatsby* is stylish, luxurious, and roomy enough for a large party. No doubt her namesake would approve.

ABOVE: Docked in New York City, this 42-foot (12.8m) deckhouse cruiser is only a few miles away from the Bayonne, New Jersey shipyards where she was built

RIGHT: *Miss Charlotte* is a 35-foot (10.6m) Elco Sportfish, perfect for overnight fishing trips off the Florida coast.

OPPOSITE: This large custom cruiser was built in 1946 in Victoria, British Columbia, by Falconer Marine Limited. She was completely overhauled in 1975.

Owens developed in their hull designs. They advertised as America's number one cruiser and it's easy to see why. Powered by 100- to 300-horsepower engines, these boats reached speeds of up to 25 mph (40kph). The flagship of the fleet, the 42-foot (12.8m) Flying Bridge, powered by twin Packard Eights, was described this way in the company's advertising:

> *The Owens 42' Flying Bridge is characterized by functional styling. It has dual controls, large convenient deck cabins, comfortable inner spring beds for seven in four private compartments, with two lavatories one of which is equipped with a shower, an abundance of locker space for hanging clothes and storage of other equipment. There is a dining nook with refrigerator, alcohol bottled gas stove, and concealed fluted glass dish rack.*

Wheeler Shipyard Co. of Clason Point, New York, had been building boats since 1914, distributing vessels that ranged from 22-foot (6.7m) Sea Skiffs to the 72-foot (22m) Promenade Deck Cruiser. In 1950 they offered boats and yachts from 28 to 55 feet (8.5–16.8m). The Playmate Sedan series included a 30-footer (9.2m), which had accommodations for four, a large galley, separate heads, and speeds of up to 20 mph (32kph). The 33-footer (10m) slept six in two separate cabins, and was available with single or twin screws. The 40-foot (12.2m) Sedan was one of their more comprehensive models, including running water, stainless steel galley, shower, teak cockpit, foam rubber mattresses, sleeping space for seven, and the ability to make speeds of 25 mph (40kph).

ABOVE: The distinctive Chris-Craft logo evokes many memories of sun, fishing, and happy times.

The 46-foot (14m) Fly Bridge Yacht had excellent accommodations. There were four separate cabins, three heads, shower, large galley, closets, and many other features. The top of the line in 1950 was the 55-foot (16.8m) Promenade Deck Yacht. This lushly appointed yacht boasted accommodations that included a main salon, two spacious staterooms, two heads with shower, dinette suite, crews' quarters for two, a large galley, and plenty of closets and bureaus. Topsides, a main flush deck ran from the bow to within 6 feet (1.8m) of the stern, protected on all sides by deck rails. They were available with either twin screw gas or diesel, depending on individual preference.

Chris-Craft, of course, had a line of luxury yachts that were very smart and very competitive. Although production-line built, the Constellation line of yachts, for example, were quite spacious and featured many amenities. The 45-foot (13.7m) Constellation with optional diesels could easily sleep eight. Virtually the entire boat from bow to stern was enclosed, creating an impressive living and entertaining area. The steering station was on the top deck, along with a large open expanse of deck for fun in the sun and general shenanigans. The 50-foot (15.2m) Constellation was virtually the same as the 42-footer (12.8m), but also sported a bridge enclosure with a streamlined hardtop and sliding glass side shields. The 55-footer (16.8m) incorporated another special addition—an aft cockpit for fishing with steps up to the main deck and access into the aft cabin. Power was provided by twin gas or diesels that together yielded 600 horsepower and maintained speeds of 25 mph (40kph). With three separate heads and the ability to sleep ten, this cruiser was one well-appointed yacht. The 65-foot (19.8m) Constellation was very similar to its smaller sister ship, but excluded the aft cockpit and added another head. Teak fore and aft decks connected by wide, protected side decks offered more than 600 square feet (183 square m) of space for living the high life. Clearly, this was a vessel that catered to those who knew what they wanted and had the means to get it.

Chris-Craft's advertisement for this luxurious cruising yacht sums it up:

Never before have shipbuilders produced a more magnificent tribute to their art than the 65ft Chris-Craft Motor Yacht. Designed for the discriminating yachtsman, it reflects the spaciousness, luxury, and appointments of contemporary tri-level living. The pilothouse offers a clear view around the horizon; the wide forward deck is ideal for sunning; and the canopied aft deck offers ample room to relax with friends. Indoors, the fashionable deckhouse salon has the gracious appointments which contribute to casual, easy-going shipboard living. There's a complete galley and separate dining salon; owner's stateroom and two guest staterooms, each with private toilet; a captain's cabin, crews' quarters and dining area. Special features can be incorporated at extra cost.

Recreational boating meant, of course, more than waterskiing, cruising, and racing. An elite portion of the market wanted to go deep-sea fishing and required vessels that met the very specific demands of the open water. Fly bridges, large open aft cockpits, mounted fighting chairs, twin engines for reliability, and minimal amenities allowed the sport fisher to hunt the mighty marlin and other big game fish. Ernest

Hemingway, one of the most recognizable figures to indulge in this obsession, represents the wealthy adventurer who cruised off the Caribbean in search of the ultimate catch. Many builders were producing sportfishers; Wheeler, Chris-Craft, and Hatteras were some of the major yards that turned out a variety of this type of vessel.

The Wheeler Shipyard Co. of Toms River, New Jersey, had been producing boats in all sizes starting in 1931. In 1950 they produced a 40-foot (12.2m) Sportfisher from their standard Wheeler sedan hull. Fitted with a flying bridge, dual controls, pulpit crow's nest, and fishing chairs, and powered by twin Chryslers that easily reached speeds of 20 mph (32kph), this was a real fishing machine. With a very long bow and a generally "modified" feel to them, the first attempts were a little awkward looking, as if these items had just been slapped on an enclosed cruiser with steering on the roof.

Wheeler offered five Sportfishers in their fleet for 1950, ranging in size from 28 to 44 feet (8.5–13.4m). All included pulpits, fishing masts, outriggers, fish tanks, fishing chairs, and a large swim grid. After a few years of design work the company finally smoothed the extras into the hull and began producing Sportfishers that looked like the models we know today. Soon the Sportfishers out of this shop were dedicated fish hunters with all the conveniences of home on board, including head, small galley, and sleeping accommodations.

The majority of Sportfishers that could really get to the marlin were over the 40-foot (12.2m) length but there were companies producing smaller vessels. In 1959 Chris-Craft produced two Sportfish models, a 33 1/2-footer (10.2m) and a 40-foot (12.2m) model. The 1959 33 1/2-foot (10.2m) Sportfish has always been one of Jim's favorites. For a number of years now he has been lucky enough to own one—*The Huntress*—a beautiful example of this type of vessel, finished in fifties-style aqua and white. *The Huntress* has hosted many memorable moments for both of the authors. Justus in particular recalls a very early summer morning when he was woken from a dead sleep in his tent on the shore of one of British Columbia's Gulf Islands, poked his bleary head out of the flaps, and was very startled to see *The Huntress* screaming past the campsite on full plane with one James Ogilvie Knowles dancing about on the flybridge, laying into the horn for all he was worth. Amazing what one can get up to at 8 a.m. on a Sunday morning. . . .

BELOW: Chris-Craft sea skiffs such as this 1961 27-footer (8.2m) were made with the sport fisherman in mind. They were roomy yet practical, with enough power to carry in a big haul.

Epilogue

MODERN DAY

THE LEGACY CONTINUES

The influence of the woody is still felt today in a number of ways. The longevity of a classic woody properly maintained means that thousands of these vessels still exist and are cared for by owners who appreciate their grace and beauty. It is true that fiberglass and other resins (such as epoxy) are wonderful building materials. They are light, almost infinitely malleable, strong, and relatively inexpensive. To the lover of wood, however, they are still really just "plastic." For some, the continued interest in and, in some cases, obsession with these classic wooden motorboats is a reaction against fiberglass and the values it represents. Plastic is cheap and disposable, modern and high tech. It is low maintenance and maximum flash. Wood, on the other hand, is natural and old—it has a history. It can be very expensive and it demands care and attention. In a word, wood has romance. Some present-day companies have recognized this backlash and are again producing wooden inboards using the traditional methods. These efforts are still quite small and localized, with the majority producing custom-made craft to order that are in a class all their own.

The individuals who own and love these classics are their own breed as well. Two breeds, really, if the experience of the authors is anything to go by. One school of woody owners is from the older generation. These are men and women who grew up around wooden boats and have fond memories of them from their past. For this group, woodies are nostalgic vessels—maintaining and operating is a labor of love because they reaffirm the old-fashioned values of work, pride, and good clean fun. The other school is younger, greener, but no less impassioned or committed. These are people who have grown up in this fast-paced, commercial, materialistic society of ours and have selected another option. For them the woody represents a return to a simpler and more honest way of living, one that is less crass and more genuine. These types of woody owners seem to be the most likely to actually live aboard their boats, reaffirming their concept of the woody as symbolic of an entire lifestyle. Of course, there are always those among us who simply think the classic woodies are beautiful, and there's no arguing with that line of reasoning.

S o u r c e s

Antique Boat Connection
5521 Vine Street
Cincinnati, OH 45217
United States
www.antiqueboat.com

The Antique and Classic Boat
  Society
422 James Street,
Clayton, NY 13624
United States
www.acbs.org

Antique Outboard Motorboat
  Club, Inc.
Department IN
PO Box 69
Sussex, WI 53089
United States
www.aomci.org

Bristol Classics Limited
2511 State Highway 7
Excelsior, MN 55331
United States
www.bristol-classics-ltd.com

The Center for Wooden Boats
1010 Valley Street
Seattle, WA 98109
United States
www.cwb.org

Chris Craft
8161 15th Street East
Sarasota, FL 34243
United States
www.omc-online.com/
chriscraft/chriscrafthome

Chris-Craft Antique Boat
  Club, Inc.
217 South Adams Street
Tallahassee, FL 32301
United States
www.chris-craft.org

Classic Boatworks of Maine
HC 77 Box 237A
Hancock, ME 04640
United States
www.nemaine.com/
classicboatworks/

Classic Marine
10275 Old Placerville Road #4
Sacramento, CA 95827
United States
www.angelfire.com/ca/classicmarine

Classic Yacht Association
149-B West Ave.
San Clemente CA 92672
United States
www.classicyacht.org

Elco
16 Shadyside Road
Ramsey, NJ 07466
United States

Elliott Bay Steam Launch
  Company & Boat House
  Books
6744 S.E. 36th Avenue
Portland, OR 97202
United States
www.steamlaunch.com

Gar Wood Boat Company
129 Columbia Street
Cohoes, NY 12047
United States

The Gar Wood Society
PO Box 6003
Syracuse, NY 13217
United States
www.garwood.com

Genco Marine
544 King Street NW
Toronto, ON M5V LM3
United States

Gordon Bay Marine
RR1, Hwy 169
MacTier, ON P0C 1HO
Canada

Hacker Boat Company
PO Box 2576
United States
Silver Bay, NY 12874

Huckins Yacht Corporation
3482 Lakeshore Boulevard
Jacksonville, FL 32210
United States

Kitsilano Marine Supply
1648 Druanleau Street
Vancouver, BC 921 7476
Canada

Lyman Boat Owners
  Association
499 Foxborough Drive
Brunswick, OH 44212
United States
www.lymanboatownersassoc.org

The Mariners' Museum
100 Museum Drive
Newport News, VA 23606
United States
www.mariner.org

Muskoka Fine Watercraft
Port Carling, Ontario P0B 1JO
Canada

The Nautical Mind
249 Queen's Quay West
Toronto, ON M5J 2N5
Canada

The Rigging Shop
44 Midwest
Scarborough, ON M1P 3A9
Canada

Southern Crown Boatworks
3157 Presidential Drive
Suite 203
Atlanta, GA 30340
United States
http://www.
southerncrownboatworks.com

Wooden Boat Association of
  Queensland Inc.
PO Box 10523
Brisbane, Queensland
Australia
www.ozemail.com.au/~woodboat

Wooden Boat Associations of
  New South Wales
PO Box 586
Drummoyne
New South Wales 2047
Australia

Wooden Boat Foundation
Cupola House
380 Jefferson Street
Port Townsend, WA 98368
United States
www.olympus.net/wbf

WoodenBoat Publications Inc
PO Box 78, Naskeag Road
Brooklin, Maine 04616
United States

For more information and
links to suppliers, restorers,
and builders, visit the
author's website at
www.woodiesrunabouts.net

I n d e x

Photo Credits